ROD GREEN

MAN UP!

ROD GREEN
MAN UP!

THE REAL MAN'S BOOK OF MANLY KNOWLEDGE

Illustrated by Andrew Pinder

Michael O'Mara Books Limited

Grateful thanks to Dan Smith, David Woodroffe, Andrew Pinder, Ana Bježančević, Greg Stevenson, Kate Gribble, and Glen Saville – all of whom acted with cool heads and steady nerves.

First published in this edition in Great Britain in 2013 by
Michael O'Mara Books Limited
9 Lion Yard
Tremadoc Road
London SW4 7NQ

Papers used by Michael O'Mara Books Limited are natural, recyclable products made from wood grown in sustainable forests. The manufacturing processes conform to the environmental regulations of the country of origin.

ISBN: 978-1-78243-030-8 in hardback print format
ISBN: 978-1-78243-031-5 in EPub format
ISBN: 978-1-78243-032-2 in Mobipocket format

5 7 9 10 8 6

Designed and typeset by www.glensaville.com
Printed and bound by CPI Group (UK) Ltd, Croydon, CR0 4YY
www.mombooks.com

CONTENTS

Emergency First Aid

Dealing with Animals

Coping with the Unexpected

Dressing the Part

Introduction

Men, are you tiring of the sedentary pleasures of the modern world? Are you wearied by web surfing? Bored of the vicarious thrills offered by the shoot-'em-ups and racing games on your console? Jaded by life among the MTV generation, so that even the videos of Lady Gaga do nothing for you now?

Of course, there are many things in today's world for which the modern man should be truly thankful – takeaway pizza, sat-nav, five-blade disposable razors, painless dentistry and Cheryl Cole, to name but a few. But they have come at a price – our ability to go out and create our own adventures and to deal with danger. However, your ennui is telling. I do declare that you are ready to write your own stories of derring-do and to reconnect with a more noble past where a boy grew up learning all the skills needed to be a real chap.

Not so long ago, our fathers and grandfathers could light fires in the rain, deal with a blown-out tyre, replace a missing button, come up with a tasty supper out in the wilds, even land a light aircraft in an emergency. In short, they knew how to do lots of things that so many men today simply don't have a clue about. Yet, this pool of invaluable knowledge was not garnered at special secret evening classes or from a sweep of the internet, nor were boys born with it somehow pre-built into their DNA.

So how did they come to know the best way to deal with an angry bull or to save a drowning man? Well, many of them picked up know-how during a childhood in the Scout movement (back in the days when health-and-safety regulations had not begun to strangle us). Still more skills were drilled into them or learned by necessity when they were serving their country in the armed forces. The rest was simply passed on from father to son.

Add to this the fact that young men now travel further to college, university and work. Gone are the days when many a son neither expected nor wanted anything more than to follow his father into the local factory or down the local pit. In itself, that is no bad thing, and how many of those old factories or pits are still there anyway? But with them went a great deal of tradition, including the gradual passing on of life skills from one generation to another.

This book cannot replace that sacred relationship, but within its pages you will find a plethora of hints and tips not only on how to cope when you have to face up to things without the help of modern technology, but also on how and why you should learn some of those important little gems that a young man of years past would almost certainly have known – with some twenty-first-century twists thrown in for good measure.

The skills that will serve you best are universal. First, you must always keep a calm head. Getting into a stew never helped anybody. Secondly, you must prepare yourself as best you can for what lies ahead. That does not mean that you won't find yourself in a situation somewhere along the line that is wholly unexpected, and that is where your calm head will come in. However, ahead of most expeditions you can equip yourself for a great number of the eventualities that you might meet.

Naturally, what you should have in your kit will depend very much on the particular circumstances of your trip and the environment in which you will be exploring. There are a few staples that should serve you well almost anywhere though. Chief among these are suitable food and drink supplies, compact enough to fit in your kit bag and full of the energy and nutrients you need. Water or sports drinks will always serve you better than alcohol or sugary pop. A survival bag – a man-sized plastic bag that folds up very small – can be used not only to preserve body heat, but also as the roof of a bivvy and for a variety of other purposes.

A few other tools are of obvious value. For instance: a torch, a button compass, a distress whistle, a first-aid kit and water-purification tablets. A flint-and-steel, matches and a birthday cake candle will give you the power of fire, while a tampon (yes, you have read correctly) can provide you with a compact supply of tinder. And what of condoms? They are not carried simply in the hope that a chap might get lucky in the woods. A non-lubricated prophylactic will stretch inside a spare sock to make a useful water carrier. It can also keep essential items dry (such as matches) and is elastic enough to be used as the sling in a rudimentary catapult (which could have given an adult spin to all those *Just William* stories).

Some cord (or twine or string) will come in useful as a means of lashing or for a rudimentary fishing kit, while a stout stick is worth its weight in gold (as is a really decent pocket-knife, but take due notice of the law relating to carrying knives). Not only does a stick offer a source of support, but you can use it to check the ground in front of you, clear away undergrowth, reach out to someone in distress, repel a predator, knock wooden stakes into the ground, dispatch a snared rabbit . . . the list goes on. And never, ever underestimate the value of a sturdy and comfy pair of brogues.

You may now begin your education in earnest.

Skills for the Great Outdoors

I f you're going to take yourself off on an adventure, there are a number of simple skills that you can practise before-hand. In the event that something on your trip then goes awry, you have a sound knowledge base to call upon. Whether you simply want to relive your Scouting days or plan to be an SAS commando, you can do no better than to be prepared. The following skills are ones that should serve you well no matter what sort of environment you are in.

How to Make Your Own Compass

To be lost is to be in danger. That is why any right-thinking gent will double-check his kit pre-jaunt to make sure he has packed all the maps that he might need and a compass to boot. But what if you do find yourself in the back of beyond without any of the basic tools to tell you where you are or which way to go? Well, all is not lost (even if you are) as you can use some old-fashioned initiative to find your bearings.

What You'll Need

A wristwatch (analogue, not digital)
The sun

How to Do It

This clever little strategy works because, while the sun rises in the east and sets in the west no matter where you are in the world, you can also use the sun to establish your north and south. If you happen to be in the northern hemisphere, at the strike of twelve the sun is due south. If you are in the southern hemisphere, it will be due north.

But your watch can serve as a compass at any daylight hour. If you are in the northern hemisphere, make sure your wristwatch is perfectly horizontal and target the hour hand at the sun. The point that lies halfway between twelve o'clock and the hour hand is due south. If you repeat the same procedure south of the Equator, the midway point will be due north.

In the absence of an analogue watch, simply draw a clock face on a piece of paper. Check the time from another source (say a digital watch or a mobile phone) and draw the hands on to your paper. Unless you are wonderfully skilful with a pencil, it won't be quite as accurate, but will do the job in an emergency.

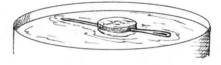

An alternative way of creating your own compass requires you to get your hands on a sewing needle of an inch or two in length, a small magnet, a piece of cork (ideally from a wine bottle) and a small container (such as a glass) filled with water. Rub the needle with the magnet for a minute or so, always stroking the magnet in the same direction. When the needle is magnetized, push it through your cork so that about the same length of needle is exposed on either side. Float the cork-and-needle on the surface of the water in your container, which you will have placed on level ground. The needle will then 'search out' the nearest pole, north or south, depending on where in the world you are, and point in that direction. Ingenious, although if you have all the necessary kit to hand, one might consider why you didn't pack a spare compass in your kit instead. Nor should you down a bottle of wine just to liberate a cork. Not only is it a waste but you'll probably end up skewering your finger with the needle too.

How to Read a Compass

If you have been sensible enough to pack an orienteering compass, well done! However, where once we could be sure that any male capable of tying his own shoelaces would also know how to use this most basic instrument, we can make no such assumptions today. You will obviously not wish to admit this in public but we shall have no secrets here. Here's how to do it.

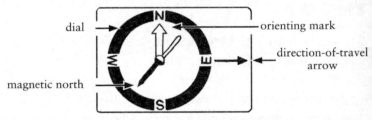

Hold your compass flat. The needle will probably have one end painted red. After a few moments, this end of the needle will settle in one position, pointing to magnetic north. While keeping the compass flat, you can now twist the dial so the orienting mark for north is in line with the red end of the needle. All the other main compass points will now be automatically aligned. Make sure you are not in the vicinity of any large metal objects or magnets of any size, as these will affect the readings and guarantee that you get lost.

How to Navigate with the Sun

Should you lack the necessary apparatus for either of these above methods, you can still establish where north and south are using only what nature gives you (and a little bit of string).

What You'll Need

A long, straight stick
Two pebbles of average size
A patch of level ground
A length of string
A twig
A few spare hours

How to Do It

1) In the morning, drive the stick into the ground and place one of the pebbles at the far edge of the shadow it casts.

2) Tie one end of your string to the base of the stick and the other end to the twig, which you are going to use as an impromptu pencil. Draw a semi-circular arc round the stick at the same distance as the pebble you have put down.

3) As time passes, the stick will cast gradually shorter shadows in the run-up to midday and then longer ones again. When the tip of the shadow exactly hits the arc you have drawn, mark the spot with the second pebble.

4) A straight line between your morning pebble and evening pebble reflects the east–west passage of the sun in reverse.

That is to say, your morning pebble is 'west' and the evening pebble is 'east'.

5) Now you know where east and west are, simply draw a bisecting line to represent north and south.

Have you got all that? It's simple, really, but rather time-consuming, and no good if you want to get away in a hurry.

How to Navigate with the Stars

Man has used the stars to navigate for thousands of years. However, it is not an easy skill to learn (especially in an age when sat-nav systems have dulled our navigational senses still further) and it would take many years of study to commit all of the secrets of the stars to memory. However, you should be able to remember a few basic facts that might just save you one dark and stormy night . . .

Remember, the passage of the Earth means that the sky can look very different from one night to another, with constellations seeming to change position. Nor should you expect to see the same thing in the northern as in the southern hemisphere. In fact you'll need to adopt quite different strategies.

How to Find 'North' in the Northern Hemisphere

The key here is the North Star (also known as Polaris), one of the brightest stars in the sky and one that, thankfully, never seems to move. Its great use to us lies in the fact that it rests above the North Pole. In order to find it, you will need to identify the Plough (or Big Dipper) constellation.

Look at the diagram above. It does not take a Galileo to tell you that, rather than a plough, this looks much more like a frying pan with a giant handle. To locate Polaris, take the two stars that make up the pan's far edge and follow the line up about six times the length that lies between them.

For an east–west line, you'll need Orion (or the Hunter). Again, this constellation is distinguished by its lack of similarity to any hunter you're ever likely to have seen. However, it does incorporate a line of three reasonably easy-to-spot stars that make up Orion's Belt. This line will give you a rough east-west guideline, so it is worth learning how to find Orion.

How to Find 'South' in the Southern Hemisphere

Unhelpfully, Polaris is not visible south of the equator. Instead you'll make use of the Southern Cross constellation. Remarkably, at its centre are four stars that do indeed form a recognizable cross. To find the Southern Cross, you must locate an area of the Milky

Way known as the Coal Sack, which is essentially a dark area of sky. In this area you can see the four stars just described plus a fifth, fainter one. To the left of this arrangement are two bright, pointer stars and to its right another cross of four dimmer stars (which you can simply ignore). Follow the line down between the top and bottom points of the Southern Cross and continue this imaginary line for a further four-and-a-half times its length. Then drop your gaze down to the horizon and you will have located due south. The diagram also shows a line projected at right angles to a line linking the two pointer stars, which, if extended in the same way, also indicates south.

How to Signal You're in Trouble

It might just be that no amount of navigation is going to get you out of a corner. Perhaps you find yourself in an area that is too inhospitable to risk moving around, or you or a colleague may be injured. In that case, you will need to signal your distress to attract help.

In an ideal world you will have a working mobile phone, but when you can't rely on your service provider coming up with a signal in your downstairs front room, it would be foolhardy to expect that it will do so in the middle of a dense forest or the desert.

Alternatively, you might have had the foresight to pack some flares. They might be slightly bulky, but isn't that a price worth paying for something that could save your life? A whistle can also be invaluable if you need to attract the attention of local passers-by. Mother Nature is able to provide plenty of signal-making tools too, which suggests she may be rather more sympathetic to the ill-prepared than she ought to be. And let us be thankful for that!

The key message to remember will do the trick in virtually any corner of the world – SOS (allegedly, Save Our Souls). You might write this on the ground using sticks in the hope that an aircraft or someone on foot will see it. Alternatively, you can render it in Morse code (by three dots, three dashes and threes dots). You could do this using a torch or by blasts on a whistle. Or you could use a mirror to reflect the sun's rays towards a passing aircraft, covering the mirror at suitable points to spell out your message.

You may also put your trust in a fire, particularly at night-time. A fire will make you visible on the ground and to those in the air. Fresh green foliage added to the fire will produce dense smoke, which in daylight you could use to give out an SOS smoke signal.

Should you be transmitting by radio, the call of Mayday (from the French *'m'aider'* or 'help me') is internationally recognized. And if you are in trouble on a mountain, the international mayday call consists of six flashes of a torch light, six blasts on a whistle, or a minute of waving something eye-catching, followed by another minute of silence. Acknowledgement of your plea for help will come via three flashes, blasts or waves.

Remember, those who come to rescue you are likely to be risking themselves in the process. Be grateful and, if needs be, a little humble. When you embarked on your adventure, you may well have felt like James Bond, but in truth you might have been more like Mr Bean. In such cases, tea and sympathy is just too much to expect.

How to Climb a Tree

You might have any number of reasons to climb a tree. Perhaps it is to gain a good vantage point for surveying the local area, or to pick a particularly scrumptious-looking fruit. Or maybe to escape a ferocious animal (or, it has been known on occasion, a jealous husband . . .). Sometimes, *à la* George Mallory and Mount Everest, you are overcome by the desire to climb one simply because it is there. Throughout history it has been a classic rite of male passage to shin up a tree, but it is worth remembering a few basic rules to ensure such an escapade does not end in disaster.

What You'll Need

A sturdy tree
An equally sturdy pair of shoes and sensible clothing

How to Do It

1) Make sure you are suitably attired. Footwear should really be of the laced variety, double-knotted, and have good grip. Similarly, clothing should be snug-fitting, reducing the risk inherent in baggy clothes of getting caught on a branch. A tough fabric can protect your skin should you experience slippage on the tree trunk. A pair of gloves with good grip can also be beneficial, but make sure you can still 'feel' the tree through them.

2) Choose your tree with care. First and foremost, make sure it is strong enough to support someone of your size. (A good reason not to scoff too many cakes just before a climb.) Have a look round the base of the trunk for piles of fallen branches and twigs. If you find lots, it may well be that the tree is rotting and you should search out a different one. Keep an eye open for poison ivy or any nasty bugs, which you should most assuredly avoid. And do not choose a tree with lots of evidence of animal or bird habitation. Climbing a tree is meant to be a chance to commune with nature, not to destroy it!

3) Warm up. As with all types of exercise, you want to make sure your muscles are ready for the challenges ahead. Some simple stretches can ensure you don't pay the price of a climb for days to come.

4) Start your climb by using a strong, low branch to pull yourself

up into the tree. Make sure you have a good foothold too. As you ascend, always use strong-looking branches to hold on to. Branches are always strongest where they meet the trunk. A flimsy branch that snaps off in your hand or beneath your feet will bring the mission to an early and unhappy end.

5) Do not rush. You need to work with the tree but not let it become your master. Climb predominantly with your legs, which is less exhausting than relying on your arms. Patiently search out the safest route to the top. If you cannot identify such a passage, you will need to abort.

6) Once you have reached the top, prepare yourself mentally for the descent. You should stay facing the trunk on the way down, just as you did on the way up. If you can, retrace your route. Do not peer too far down as this may result in an attack of vertigo. And do not be tempted to leap off, even if you feel like you're almost down on the ground. It would be a dreadful pity to end a successful climb with a pointless sprain or worse.

How to Stay Safe from Lightning

If you are going to be a conductor, make sure it is of a symphony orchestra and not of electricity. There is precious little to be gained from being the victim of a lightning strike. It is true that if your time has come, there is not much you can do about it, but you can certainly make provision to keep the risk as low as possible.

While most of us see lightning only every now and again, there can be as many as 1,000 thunderstorms happening around the world at any one time, lighting up the sky with up to ten flashes of lightning per second. Lightning occurs when warm air, heated by the sun or by the warmth of earth or water that has been exposed to the sun, rises. The cold air that drops down from a higher altitude through the warm air itself warms up, creating a convection cycle of air currents.

The rising and falling air currents cause friction between particles in the air, and also between particles of moisture in a cloud. All of this friction causes a negative electrical charge to form at the bottom of the cloud and a positive charge at the top. From time to time there will be a short circuit, just as you would get when you touch together two wires attached to the terminals of a battery. Normally the spark will occur within the cloud or jump from one cloud to another. But if the negative charge at the bottom of the cloud is offered an easier way to discharge, such as jumping to the ground, then we see lightning.

How Dangerous is a Strike?

A lightning bolt may be only about two inches (5cm) in diameter but it produces an intense heat of more than 33,000°C and enough electricity to power the average light bulb for three months. Lightning will find the easiest route to earth, jumping the gap – or arcing – between the sky and the ground by using a high point such as a church spire or a tall tree. If it is you that provides the 'easiest route', you will be very lucky to escape serious injury. Around the world, it is estimated that almost 2,000 people are hit by lightning every year, with up to a third of them being killed.

How to Avoid a Lightning Strike

The heat produced by the electrical discharge causes the air around a lightning bolt to expand, creating a kind of shock wave that we hear as thunder. When you hear loud thunder, you know that there is the likelihood of lightning activity nearby.

You can judge how far away a lightning storm is by counting the number of seconds between the flash of lightning and the clap of thunder. The speed of sound is roughly 1,100 feet per second. That is equivalent to around one fifth of a mile per second. Count the number of seconds between the flash and the thunder, divide by five and you will know approximately how many miles away the storm is. If you count less than 30 seconds, then you know that the storm is less than six miles away. That means it could be with you at any moment and you should find a safe shelter.

If you are caught out in the open in a thunderstorm, you should avoid any high places, stay well clear of any tall metal structures and do not shelter under a tree. If it is raining, on no account use an umbrella. Stay away from metal fences. If you are fishing, ditch your state-of-the-art superconducting, carbon-fibre rod no matter how much it cost you. If you are out golfing, abandon your game. Raising a length of metal above your head to play a golf shot is really asking for trouble.

Do not seek shelter in a tin hut, a golf cart or an open-topped car. If a closed car or truck is hit by lightning, you will be safe inside, but avoid touching any bare metal surfaces. Nor are tents with metal poles good places to be in a thunderstorm. Your best protection will be in a cave or in a large building. A big building will provide the best protection, but even there you should stay away from metal window frames, telephone landlines, computer terminals, TVs or any other electrical appliances.

What If There Is No Shelter?

If you are out in the open, swimming in a lake or river or crossing a flat tract of land, follow these rules:

1) Stay calm. You are more likely to injure yourself in an accident by panicking than you are to be hit by lightning.
2) If you are swimming, get out of the water.
3) Crouch or squat on the ground. Do not lie on the ground. If there is a ground strike, your shoes can insulate you, so squat as low as you can with only the soles of your feet touching the ground.
4) Do not seek shelter in a ditch, trench or hollow. You could become the bridge that the lightning uses to leap the gap.
5) Do not run around. A lightning bolt travels at thousands of miles per hour. That is to say, faster than you!
6) Be patient. Thunderstorms do not tend to last very long and the danger will have passed within a few minutes of you having heard the last thunderclap.

How to Conquer a Can without an Opener

For a man to stay safe in the wilds, he'll need a full belly and a happy heart. What you don't want to do is let yourself get hungry, which will leave you feeling weak and tired and lacking in judgement. Imagine the scene, then, in which you have made the effort to pack sensible supplies of tinned food only to discover that you've forgotten to bring a can opener. Don't panic, though.

You'll be feasting soon enough as long as you can lay your hands on a decent knife. Now don't say you've forgotten that too . . .

Place the can on a flat surface and hold it tightly around the middle in your non-dominant hand. With the knife in your other hand and the point aimed away from you, make a quick stab into the lid, near the edge, so that it penetrates about half an inch. You must then use the knife to hack away round the edge of the lid until it will open sufficiently. Your grasp on the body of the tin must not loosen and you should undertake the whole process with complete concentration. Use the knife (not your hand) to prise open the lid, and once you have finished with the contents, put the jagged can out of harm's way. In the absence of a knife, you should be able to open a can simply by repeatedly sweeping the end of the can over a flat, abrasive surface, such as the top of a rock, with enough pressure to wear away the tin's lip, thus allowing you to open the lid.

How to Beat a Bottle Top

Worried you might have a drinking problem? Is the problem that you forgot your bottle opener? Here's how to get round it.

Take a five-pound note, fold it in half and then roll it as tight as possible. Fold it in half again so that it forms a bend and then wedge the point under the bottle top. The rolled note should sit between your thumb and index finger. Hold the neck of the bottle with your non-dominant hand. Push the note up and, hey presto, the top should pop off. In fact, it will be propelled with such force that you should probably warn any onlookers.

Alternatively, you could use a belt buckle, placing one edge tightly over the cap of the bottle. Use your thumb on the other edge of the buckle, pushing hard. It should work just like a traditional bottle-opener.

A wine bottle can be opened with similar ease, even in the absence of a corkscrew. You can cobble together a makeshift one of your own out of two paper clips. In the first instance, straighten the clips out, but make sure you leave the U-shapes intact. Take your first clip and slip it into the neck of the bottle, small 'u' first, in the gap between glass and cork. Once the 'u' is below the base of the cork, give it a quarter-turn twist so that its point works its way into the cork when you pull the other end of the paper clip. Repeat with the second clip on the opposite side of the cork. When they are both locked in place, unwind the big 'u's and entwine them. You will have a corkscrew just strong enough for the job.

And remember, to avoid extreme embarrassment, you should always first make sure that your bottles do not have screw tops.

How to Pick a Lock

If you've managed to lock yourself out of your accommodation – a remote mountain hut, say – or perhaps the key to your backpack lock has gone astray, you can pay out a great sum of money for the services of a locksmith (assuming you can find one). Alternatively, you can unlock the cat burglar within yourself.

What You'll Need

An improvised pick
An improvised tension wrench

How to Do It

1) In the first instance, figure out what sort of lock you're dealing with. Many everyday locks are of the pin-and-tumbler variety. These work by way of a cylinder within a housing, which when locked is kept in place by several pairs of pins (kept in situ with springs), of which the upper pin protrudes into the cylinder at one end and into housing at the other.

2) The correct key will push the pins up and out of the cylinder, allowing it to be turned and the lock opened. It is this effect that you will need to replicate.

3) Assuming you don't have a set of manufactured picks and

tension wrenches on you, you will need to make them yourself. (In many territories, having your own set is not considered *de rigueur* and may bring you to the attention of the local constabulary.) The tension wrench will be inserted into the bottom of the lock to manoeuvre the cylinder. The pick works at the top of the lock to set the pins away from the cylinder. For a tension wrench, you want something strong enough to exert pressure on the cylinder but small enough to leave enough room to manipulate the pick. A flathead screwdriver with a thin tip will work. A paper clip will do the trick as a pick. You will need to straighten the clip and then bend it at right-angles very close to one end. The clip won't see you through many jobs but it should be just about sturdy enough for the average lock.

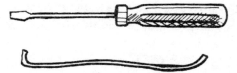

4) Insert the tension wrench and work out which way the cylinder turns. Try clockwise first, then counter-clockwise. You won't be able to get very far either way, but the direction that has the most give will be the right way.

5) Insert the pick. You will be able to sense the pins and should be able to push them up and feel them fall down again. You should then attempt to push them all the way up. One may feel more resistant than the others. If all the pins go up very easily or one won't go up at all, adjust the tension wrench to decrease or increase the torque.

6) Use just enough force to set the most stubborn pin in the

'up' position – the torque applied by your wrench slightly misaligns the cylinder, so that the upper pin cannot descend (the lower pins turn with the cylinder). When you can push the lower pin up with hardly any resistance from the spring, you may assume the pair of pins are set.

7) Repeat for all the other pins. You may have to spend some time discovering by experimentation the correct order to set the pins.

8) Once the pins have been set, you should be able to turn the cylinder with the wrench.

A skilled lock-picker will tell you that it is all in the tension wrench and making sure you have just the right torque to let you push the pins up out of the cylinder and keep them in place. Also, your eyes cannot see much in a lock but your hearing and touch can give you all sorts of indications as to what is going on inside.

Remember, this is a trick to get you out of a scrape. You alone will be responsible for whatever misfortune befalls you if you use it with anything but the most innocent intentions. You have been warned!

In the Woods

You've had a grand day yomping through the undergrowth and time has rather got away from you. There's no possible way that you can get back to civilization by nightfall, and you have no great desire to anyway. Much better to spend the night under the stars, warmed by an impromptu campfire and keeping your spirits up with a good sing-song (whether you're from the 'Ging-Gang-Goolie' school or the more modernist 'Wonderwall' brigade). But to achieve this little piece of Eden, you will need some basic skills. Read on and absorb.

How to Build a Temporary Shelter

You must not leave making your decision to set up camp too late. You will need good light to select a suitable area, collect your building materials and carry out the construction. Don't wait until it is dark, cold and quite possibly wet. You don't want to have ushered in a bout of hypothermia before you've managed to cosy in. Frighteningly, that can occur when the body temperature drops just one or two degrees below normal. A simple temporary sleeping shelter, or bivouac ('bivvy'), can be built quickly and easily providing you are properly equipped.

What You Will Need

A plastic ground sheet or 'bivvy' sheet
A few feet of string, twine or parachute cord
A sharp knife

Choosing Your Location

The site for your shelter should be on flat or gently sloping ground away from any obvious water courses to avoid being flooded out halfway through the night. You should also take note of any paths created by the regular passage of animals which might take exception to your camp. Rabbits are not a problem (bar the threat of their noisy love-making) but disgruntled cattle, deer or bears might well be.

If you intend to use existing trees to support your shelter, choose a spot where your bivvy sheet can easily be stretched between them. If the trees are too close together you won't be able to stretch your sheet tight enough; if they are too far apart, the sheet or your ties may not reach.

How to Erect the Bivouac

Your bivvy sheet need only be high enough off the ground for you to crawl in underneath, but must be high enough at the front to create a reasonable slope for any rain to run off. The front should be facing away from any wind so that rain is not blown in. Your campfire will be built near the front of your bivvy, so you should take that into consideration as well.

1) Tie a length of cord to one corner of the bivvy sheet. Some sheets will come with eyelets punched into them for just such a purpose but, if not, you should tie the corner of the sheet in a knot. You can then loop the cord behind the knot and tie it fast to stop it slipping off the sheet when it is stretched.
2) Tie the cord around the trunk or branch of a tree. If there

are no suitable trees, then you should create a support pole by finding a long, straight, fallen branch, sharpening it at one end with your knife and hammering this stake into the ground using a rock or heavy branch.

3) Repeat this process for the other front corner, stretching the sheet straight and taut. Make sure that your knots are good and secure so that the sheet won't blow away during the night.

4) Take one of the rear corners and pull it taught before securing it to a tree trunk or stake almost at ground level.

5) Do the same with the opposite rear corner. Leaving a gap between the ground and the lower edge will allow for a through-flow of air, but if a strong wind is blowing, that might not be desirable. In that case, the rear edge of the sheet can be secured on the ground and be weighted down along its length with rocks or logs.

6) Branches, logs or foliage can be stacked at the sides as required, to make the shelter more cosy.

If you have had the good sense to carry a lightweight bivvy sheet and cord in your rucksack – a load hardly likely to slow you up, after all – then you can have your shelter up and ready for use in a matter of minutes. However, if you've been caught on the hop or you want the challenge of working only with what nature can provide, you can build yourself a bivouac solely from what you have foraged. Just be sure to allow yourself some extra time and daylight.

How to Build an Eco-Friendly Bivvy

The first thing to do, just as when using a bivvy sheet, is to select a suitable site for your shelter. When using natural materials you should try to make optimum use of the terrain. A rocky outcrop, a fallen tree or a furrow in the ground (providing that it does not seem prone to filling with water) can give you a head start.

The simplest type of shelter to build is a lean-to. With a lean-to you are building a roof and a wall at the same time, creating something that will fulfil the same function as a bivvy sheet.

What You'll Need

A selection of 12 straight fallen branches, no thicker than your thumb and up to around three feet (1m) long

Two longer branches, roughly as thick as your thumb and about six feet (1.8m) long

At least two dozen thinner, more flexible, branches or twigs

A few feet of string, twine or parachute cord

A ready supply of foliage – ferns or broad-leafed foliage are best

A sharp knife

How to Do It

You need to create a framework that will be the basis for your structure, on to which you will 'thatch' the foliage.

1) If you are using a fallen log or other natural feature to support your lean-to, you can take your 12 straight branches and lean them against the support, digging the bottom ends into the ground to hold them in place. They should be spaced out around six inches (15cm) apart. If you do not have the luxury of something against which to lean your shelter, then lay the poles out on the ground, again around six inches (15cm) apart.

2) Take the two longer branches and lay perpendicular to the other poles, across the top and bottom. These need to be lashed in place with a few simple turns of string or cord, attaching them top and bottom to each of the 12 poles.

3) You now have a basic frame that you can turn into a lattice or grid by weaving the thinner twigs through the twelve poles. Try to keep each row of twigs that you weave evenly spaced along the length of the poles. The more rows of twigs you can weave into the lattice, and the closer together they are, the easier you will make the job of 'thatching' the shelter.

4) If you have no natural support for your lean-to, find two stout sticks and drive them into the ground about five feet (1.5m) apart. They will need to stand high enough to create the open side of your shelter. Two feet (60cm) should do. A rock or heavy branch will serve perfectly well as a mallet. You can now lean your lattice against these two supports, digging the bottom ends into the ground a little to make it

firm and to stop the wind from lifting it. Your sloping roof, remember, should face into any prevailing wind. Now lash the top of your lattice to the two upright stakes.

5) You are ready to begin thatching. Starting at the bottom of the lattice, push your leaves or other foliage into the weave (weaving in longer stalks will help) so that the part of the leaf that would normally be uppermost is on top and the tips of the leaves are facing down. Water will generally run off the upper part of a leaf and you want it to run down the outside of your shelter. Work your way along the bottom of the shelter to create a rough row of foliage thatch, then start a little higher up on a second row. The more time you can spend on this, the more weatherproof your bivvy will be.

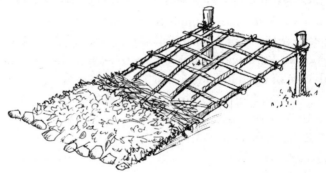

6) Once you have completed a basic thatch over the whole roof, you can place rocks along the bottom edge to hold it in place, or build up rocks or branches at the sides to help keep out the weather. You can also add to the roof anything that you have managed to scavenge from around your campsite – leafy branches, turf, plastic bags, sacking. Anything that will help to keep you dry is a good thing.

If you have no cord or string, then it is possible to weave your lattice without a properly lashed frame, but it will not be very stable. You can also strip the bark from some types of tree branch in lengths that will serve well for making lashings. In an emergency, never shy away from using a little imagination to solve problems.

How to Build and Light a Campfire

Having secured your shelter, your next priority is to build a fire. That can of beans is not going to cook itself now, is it?

A fire serves a multitude of other purposes too. Not only will it keep you warm, you will be able to dry out your clothes, signal to rescuers, purify water, make a hot drink and even ward off wild animals. It is also simply a great comfort to anyone who is stuck in a forest or on a hillside alone and an enormous boost to morale. Burrowing into your basic survival kit, you can now make use of the following items:

1) A tampon
2) A flint-and-steel
3) Matches
4) A birthday cake candle

Gentlemen, it is true, rarely have good use for a tampon, but in this instance the fine cotton wool from which it is made doubles as ideal tinder, especially when one is using a flint-and-steel. Unlike matches, which can be rendered useless if damp, or a lighter, where the flint or fuel may run out, a flint-and-steel will always produce sparks with which you can light a fire.

Matches, though, have much going in their favour and you can buy waterproof types commercially these days. Alternatively, you can spray an ordinary box and the matches themselves with hair lacquer to achieve a similar effect. But all matches suffer from the same problem in that they are one-use items and you must do everything you can to ensure that a match is not wasted. That is where the birthday cake candle comes in.

The candle is not for providing light nor is it for celebrating, even if it does happen to be your birthday – it is to help you in lighting a fire. The smallest candles are best for this. Birthday cake candles or 'tea lights' are excellent because you can afford to carry several and still fit them into a very compact survival kit. They will help to start a fire even when the tinder you are using is damp.

What You'll Need

Tinder
Kindling
Fuel
A flame or sparks

Tinder can be anything from very small twigs or shredded paper to dry moss or the cotton wool from a tampon. The essential thing is that it is totally dry. You should not need a huge amount of tinder. Kindling will be slightly larger twigs or wood shavings from dry sticks, while the fuel will be larger sticks and logs. The flame will come from your matches or flint-and-steel.

It is important that you find all of the elements you need to keep your fire going before you start trying to light it. It's no use scrabbling around looking for kindling as your tinder burns itself out. You need to have everything to hand, the fuel arranged so that you can gradually add larger sticks to the fire. You will have the opportunity to gather more fuel once your fire is well and truly lit, although you should never leave a fire untended for too long.

Preparing Your Site

You should position your fire close to the front of your bivvy, being careful not to bring it so close that sparks or flying embers will set light either to your shelter or to nearby trees or bushes. Scrape away any vegetation or fallen leaves on the ground where you intend to build your fire. The ground needs to be clear and dry. To stop the fire spreading, use a circle of stones or a barrier of damp logs around the edge of the space you have cleared. These will also act as a windbreak to stop your initial flame being blown out.

How to Light the Fire

You are now ready to build your fire and light it. You need to start by placing your kindling material in the middle of your fire site and creating a loose wigwam of kindling sticks around the kindling. Don't pile on too much kindling at this stage. Both you, with your match, and an air supply need to be able to reach the tinder.

If it has been raining, you may not have been able to find tinder or kindling that is absolutely bone dry, so it will help to use a candle. Dig a little hole in the base of your fire site and place the candle in the hole. This will stop any breeze from blowing it out. You can now build your wigwam of tinder and kindling above the candle. You can then reach in with a match to light the candle which will provide a constant flame lasting far longer than any match, and will serve to dry out the tinder and kindling until it finally catches. This may take some time in really soggy conditions, but you will get there in the end. At this stage you may be able to reach in and retrieve the candle in case it is needed again. If it is engulfed by the fire, however, or you risk upsetting your fire just as it starts to get going, leave the candle well alone. It is a small sacrifice and it has done its job.

Once your tinder is alight and your kindling has started to burn, you can add more kindling, a little at a time. Be careful not to 'swamp' the fire with wood or it will go out. The kindling and sticks that you add should be gradually larger in size until you have introduced the biggest of your sticks.

When the fire is burning nicely, you can think about adding larger fuel such as thicker branches or logs. The ring of stones or damp logs around your fire should serve to limit the size of the fire. A big fire will use up more fuel, so don't be tempted to keep piling fuel on or you will quickly run out and have to go foraging for more.

If you are using the flint-and-steel, it will shower your kindling with sparks. When one of the sparks catches, the dry kindling will start to smoulder. Gently blowing on the kindling will give it more oxygen and encourage it to burst into flame.

Other Sources of Flame

If you have no matches, lighter or flint-and-steel, there are other ways to create a spark. A magnifying glass can be used to focus the sun's rays on to your tinder or a car battery can be used to create sparks by touching together wires running from the terminals. People are often heard to say that Scouts can make fire by rubbing two sticks together. A good Cub can do a great deal but he can't do that. But you can create a flame using friction on wood.

What You'll Need

A very dry length of fallen branch
Some dry tinder
Fine kindling, very dry
A length of flexible stick as thick as your pinky and as long as your forearm
A straight piece of dry wood about as thick as your finger
A length of cord
A flat stone that will fit in the palm of your hand
A sharp knife

How to Do It

You are going to make a 'fire drill' or 'fire bow'. Take the length of flexible stick and bend it slightly, tying the cord to each end to create a bow. You now need to place your fallen branch on the ground, preferably held a little clear of a dry patch of ground supported on a couple of sticks or stones. The branch needs to be sitting stable so that it will not move about.

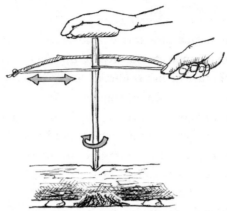

Cut a notch in the edge of the branch near the middle. Tuck some tinder directly below the notch. Now sharpen one end of your straight piece of wood as though making an arrow for your bow. Twist the arrow in the bowstring about halfway up the shaft of the arrow. Now place the point of the arrow in the notch you cut, holding it vertically but keeping the bow horizontal.

With the stone in the palm of one hand press down on the end of the arrow and saw the bow backwards and forwards with the other hand to spin the arrowhead in the notch. Get comfy because you have several hours of drilling ahead to build up enough heat for the wood and tinder to start to smoulder. Once it does, you need to blow gently on it to encourage a flame, then introduce your kindling. Never try to spin the drill by rubbing it between the palms of your hands. You will strip the skin from your hands before you have even come close to creating any heat in the wood. That is not the sort of burn we are after.

How to Find Food in the Wild

So you've got a place to shelter and a blazing fire on the go. It is only natural that your thoughts will then turn to affairs of the belly. It is said that a man can survive for up to two weeks without eating, providing that he has water, but you can be sure he won't have the energy either to plan or embark upon a journey to safety. You need to eat to maintain strength and stamina, and it does no harm to your spirit either. In a survival scenario, you may well spend the majority of your time finding sufficient food, and you must make sure that what you eat provides you with more energy than you expend looking for it. You need to know where to look for food and how to determine what is good to eat and what might make you ill.

How to Get Food from Plants

Plants can provide many essential nutrients and you will generally expend less energy sourcing food from plants than you will in hunting or trapping animals. If travelling or hiking through a region, you should take a little time to learn about the indigenous plant species, which of them are edible, and how to recognize them. Certain plants, such as fungi (including mushrooms), can be easily misidentified. Such a mistake can be deadly as some fungi are extremely poisonous to humans. Unless you are utterly confident about identifying fungi, leave them well alone.

For most other plants you can apply an edibility test (see

below). Do not attempt this with fungi, though, as the effects of a poison might not be immediately apparent. Common sense will tell you that any plant that smells bad should probably be avoided (although that is not an excuse to leave your sprouts when you're back at home). Similarly, brightly coloured plants are obligingly warning you that they are not to be eaten. Look out for local wildlife to see what plants they are eating. That which is suitable for a rabbit or squirrel may not be good for you, but the things that the locals avoid will almost certainly be bad for you.

How to Conduct an Edibility Test

The only absolutely safe way to establish whether a plant is edible or not is to know exactly what the plant is. But if you have any doubts about a plant, especially if it is abundant in your environment and would provide a plentiful source of food, then you can apply the edibility test. It's a slow process and if you have safe food alternatives, always stick to those. However, in a crisis it might just save you a lot of trouble. When your body needs to stock up on the good stuff, food poisoning is the last thing you want.

Only ever test one type of plant at a time and, as different parts of a plant may or may not be edible, you should separate the root, stem, leaves, flowers and fruit to test each in turn. Only gather healthy-looking plants from areas that look clean and free from contaminants. Wash the plants in clean water and cut away any damaged parts. Now to be a scientist, taking all the care and patience that entails.

1) The first thing to do is find out if the plant will irritate your

skin. Take a little of the material you are testing, crush it and rub it against the skin on the inside of your forearm. After half an hour, if you are not experiencing any irritation, redness, blisters or burns, move on to the next phase.

2) Crush another small piece of the test material and lodge it in your mouth between your gum and the skin below your bottom lip. Stay alert for any irritation in the mouth or nasty tastes over a period of around ten minutes.

3) If you have still had no bad reaction, try chewing the material and look out for bitterness, burning sensations or any other nasty tastes.

4) If you are still suffering no ill effects, try swallowing some of the juice from the material. Do not swallow the plant material but spit it out. Now wait for at least eight hours and be on the alert for stomach ache, sickness, cramps or any other ill effects. Do not eat anything else during this period that could interfere with the test. Do make sure that you drink fresh water as you must not become dehydrated.

5) After eight hours, assuming that you have not had any bad reaction, try eating a little of the plant, no more than the size of your thumb nail. Monitor for another eight hours.

6) If you are still feeling fine, try eating a portion of the plant no bigger than your hand. Wait for 24 hours and, if you have suffered no adverse reaction, the plant is probably safe to eat. You will most certainly deserve some sustenance after all that.

Plants that you gather for food should always be carefully washed in fresh water. Nuts, berries or fruit are often best eaten raw as they provide the optimum nutrition that way. Most other parts of a plant should be boiled to make them more palatable. Keep two containers of water on the boil and transfer the food into clean boiling water once it has been cooking for a while. Replacing the water in this way will help to lose any bitter taste in the food.

Finally, anyone interested in identifying edible plants should take time to study books and manuals on the subject and, if possible, talk to genuine experts – a mistake can be fatal.

How to Snare a Rabbit

Plant food, however plentiful, will only provide part of the nutritional needs of anyone finding themselves in a desperate situation out in the wild. Plants can ward off starvation, but you will need to eat far more vegetable matter than you normally would to keep yourself fit. This, of course, does not constitute a properly balanced diet and to maintain enough strength to survive, you will need to find animal food as well.

The following section is, I fear, not one likely to appeal to the vegetarians amongst you. Snaring a rabbit or other wildlife is not a thing to be taken lightly. It is against the law in some places and thoroughly disapproved of in others. Killing wildlife is something that should only be considered in a desperate survival situation. But if it comes down to you or Thumper . . .

The first thing to do is to make careful observations. Look for rabbit burrows in grassy embankments or near tree roots. Be vigilant for tell-tale droppings which will also help you to identify the 'runs' used by rabbits. Like most wild animals, rabbits are creatures of habit. They will set off at dusk to seek out food following the same trails that they normally use. That is why they are susceptible to snaring. Find part of a rabbit run that is well away from where you have made your camp. Your scent and the noise that you generate will scare off your prey, forcing them to use an alternative run.

How to Make a Snare

The best kind of snare is made from strong, supple wire. Basically, what you have to do is create a noose.

1) Make a small, secure loop at one end of the wire by bending a short length over and twisting it around the main length of wire.

2) Pass the other end of the wire through the loop to create a much larger loop. This is your noose. To catch a rabbit, this noose will have to be around 6½ inches (16.5cm) wide. It should slide easily, drawing close with minimal pressure.

3) The remainder of your wire must now be bent into a kind of peg that can be pushed into the ground. It needs to allow

the noose to stand vertically with the bottom of the noose around six inches (15cm) off the ground. When the rabbit comes hopping along its run, its head will go into the noose, which will tighten around its neck. (Have all the vegetarians definitely left the room?)

4) The peg is to balance the noose above the run. It needs to have another length of wire or some cord tied to it and secured to a stout wooden peg that will be driven into the ground. When the rabbit is caught in the snare, it will bound forward, but as the snare is tethered to the wooden stake, it will not be able to run off with the snare round its neck.

If you do not have any suitable wire to use as a snare, you can make one using cord or string, although obviously the noose will need to be suspended over the run in some manner, or held open using twigs. The beauty of the wire snare is that it is self-supporting and for that reason, snare wire is often included as part of a survival kit.

Positioning the Snare

You need to set your snare across the run. Rabbits typically leave heavy and light 'footprints' along their runs. You should aim to set your snare across the middle of a lighter print if you can.

Take care not to cause a disturbance when you are setting your snare and pegging it. You should try to disguise it using dead twigs. Position fallen branches either side of the run to 'channel' the rabbit into the snare. Do not cut green foliage to do this as the rabbit will either become suspicious, or will see the new foliage as a hassle-free dinner of its own.

Position your snare in the morning or early afternoon. This will allow time for the scent that you have left behind to diminish. Rubbing rabbit droppings on the snare wire will help to disguise your scent but be careful to ensure that it still works efficiently.

Checking the Trap

Do not be tempted to rush back to your trap an hour after dark to check if you have caught anything. You'll only scare off any rabbit in the vicinity. If you are setting more than one snare, keep them well apart as the commotion made by one trapped rabbit will frighten any others away.

If you have caught a rabbit in your snare and it is not dead, dispatch it straight away. To break a rabbit's neck, hold its rear legs (not just the feet) firmly in your right hand and its neck in your left. Your hand should be behind the rabbit's neck, with your thumb and forefinger reaching round below either side of the jaw. Push sharply down and twist with your left hand while pulling smartly upwards with your right. The rabbit should die immediately. Alternatively, you can whack it on the head with a rock or heavy stick, but this is not as reliable for a quick kill and can be messy.

How to Prepare a Rabbit

For the more squeamish among you, things are not going to get immediately better now you have the main ingredient for supper. You will need a sharp knife and your first task is to bleed the carcass. The easiest way to do this is to tie the rabbit's rear legs together and hang it upside down from the branch of a tree. Cut off its head with a sharp knife and let all of the blood drain out.

Hanging, gutting and skinning the rabbit are to be done as soon as possible after the kill. Because this can be a messy business, you should not do it near where you intend to reset your snare as the smell will frighten off other rabbits. Neither should you do this at your campsite because it will attract flies, scavengers and possibly envious predators. Choose a spot that is convenient for your campsite but far enough away from both your snare(s) and your camp to cause you the fewest problems.

The rabbit will bleed out quite quickly. To skin and gut it, you now need to do the following:

1) Hold the carcass with the front legs in your left hand, its back against you and its rear legs dangling down. Run your right hand down its belly towards its genitals, pushing in and down. This will empty the bladder of urine. Alternatively, you can squeeze its lower abdomen between thumb and forefinger to achieve the same effect.

2) Now use your sharp knife to make a cut from the neck all the way down the middle of the belly. Do not press too deeply. You are aiming to slice through the skin to expose the inner flesh. You need to avoid puncturing the innards.

3) Peel the skin and fur back from the belly, then carefully cut through the flesh. The innards should fall out basically intact if you give the carcass a shake but if not, you should reach inside and coax them out.

4) If you can identify the liver, kidneys, heart and lungs you may want to set these aside. These organs all look much the same in most mammals. In a survival situation, these are excellent once cooked, but if you are not confident about identifying the organs, you should discard all of the innards. Leave them in some undergrowth so that nature can recycle them. Despite how you might feel at this point, up to your elbows in rabbit guts, you don't want to be an enemy of your environment.

5) Make sure that there are no remnants from the innards left clinging to the carcass. Use your knife to scrape away anything that is not easily removed.

6) You now need to remove the skin and fur. Cut off the lower parts of each limb – the 'feet' – and cut the skin down the underside of each forelimb to the cut you previously made down its middle.

7) You can now peel the skin away from the flesh. Grip the carcass with the fingers of one hand inside the neck and work from the neck down. You may need to insert your knife blade gently between the skin and the flesh from time to time to ease the process.

8) When you have peeled the skin off all the way down to the back legs, you may have to make cuts in the back legs similar to those you made on the forelegs to help you remove the skin completely. Unless you need to spend time preparing the skin for use as emergency clothing, it should be discarded along with the

innards.

9) Trim off any small tufts of skin and fur that may still be clinging to the carcass.

10) Wash the entire carcass in fresh water, paying special attention to the body cavity to ensure that it is completely clean.

Your rabbit is now ready to be cooked, although you may choose to butcher it by cutting off the legs and shoulders. Remember that the head, ribs and other parts of the carcass can be boiled to make stock for soup, even if the bones, such as the leg, have already been roasted over your campfire. Any waste from preparing the rabbit should be burnt or buried (deep), to avoid attracting rats or even predators.

How to Tickle a Trout

Far less fluffy than the previous meal, but just as tasty, is that knight of the river, the trout. The art of tickling trout is a highly effective way of bagging supper, requiring no net, fishing rod, line, hooks or any of the normal fishing equipment. It is an old poacher's trick, which helped them avoid being prosecuted for poaching if they were caught near a landowner's trout stream. With no equipment (and their illicit catch hidden in a pocket), what could they possibly be up to? The act itself sounds like it might be faintly indecent and indeed, like snaring a rabbit, tickling a trout is illegal in some places, so check to make sure if you can proceed. Otherwise, legal or not, only use this technique if you are genuinely in trouble, and urgently need to eat.

What You'll Need

Good observational skills
Infinite patience
A delicate touch

How to Do It

Firstly, you must watch the river. Fish do not have eyelids and therefore don't like to be in bright, sunny water. See if any fish are swimming upriver from a turbulent stretch of water and making for a shady spot to rest. They are most likely to find their shade under a rock or the overhang of the riverbank. If you spy fish making for such a spot, approach with caution.

Some ticklers recommend getting into the water to have the best chance of catching the prey. That would certainly involve approaching from downstream to avoid any disturbance alerting the fish to your presence. Even so, you would still have to tread very carefully to get close enough to tickle the fish without it becoming aware of you. Other ticklers argue that you can work just as efficiently from the water's edge.

The great advantage of a fish in the shade of an overhang is that it won't be able to see you coming. Approach the spot where you think you will best be able to position yourself on the riverbank or the rock under which the fish is hiding. Lie face down on the riverbank and reach your 'tickling' hand down into the water. Make sure it is downriver from where you suspect the fish is hiding. Leave your hand and forearm in the water for a while so that they cool down closer to the water temperature.

Now very slowly and carefully, still reaching as low as you can in the water, slide your hand forward, upstream, gently feeling for the fish with the slightly cupped palm of your hand facing upwards. Make no sudden movements and stay utterly relaxed. You may have to feel your way past slippery river stones or tree roots, all of which may be covered in river slime, so this might not be the most pleasant of experiences. (Though probably better than skinning and gutting the rabbit.) Hold your nerve and if you have not handled a fish before, be prepared for the alien, slippery feel of it.

The first part of the fish you touch, ever so gently, will be its tail. Move your hand slowly along its underside and softly stroke its belly a few times before progressing slowly forward towards its gills. You may need to spend up to a minute gently stroking the belly, which relaxes the fish into a near trance-like state – a sort of sub-aqua foreplay.

Now brace yourself for a quick and fluid movement. You need to grip the fish firmly around the gills just behind the head while scooping your arm up out of the water and rolling on to your back away from the river to fling the fish on to dry land. The fish will now be utterly alert and a defiantly slippery customer. You will need to get a very firm grip on him so that he cannot wriggle free and flip back into the water. No need to worry about neck-breaking routines here; a simple smack on his head with a rock or a tree root will dispatch him swiftly.

How to Clean a Fish

Once you have successfully tickled your trout, be sure to dry off your freezing cold hands before giving yourself a hearty slap on the back and casting your mind forward to a sumptuous fishy supper. Before you can get cooking, you will need to prepare the fish, a reasonably simple job of just a few minutes. However, prepare to get your hands messy, cold and wet one final time. All you need for the job is a sharp knife.

1) Hold the fish in your left hand (right hand if you are left-handed), belly up with its head facing towards you.

2) Cut the fish open from the 'vent' (anus) near the tail to just below the gills. Be very careful when doing this, as you do not want your knife blade to go too deep and puncture the guts. This can foul the flesh and make the fish inedible.

3) Now hold the fish with your thumb under its jaw and your forefinger in its mouth. Reach into the body cavity with the fingers of your other hand and pull out all of the innards.

4) Scrape out the body cavity with your thumb to make sure that you have removed everything completely.

5) Thoroughly wash out the body cavity in clean, running water. The stream or river where you caught your fish is probably the best place.

6) Your fish can be cooked and eaten with its scales still attached but will be more enjoyable without. To scale the fish, hold it firmly by the tail and scrape your knife blade along its body from tail to head. Using the back or blunt edge of the knife will help to avoid you accidentally chopping into the fish.

7) Give a final rinse in the stream and it is ready to cook.

Your fish will best be cooked over your campfire unfilleted and with the head and tail left on. However, if you choose to remove the bones, head and tail, they can all be boiled to make a stock or used raw (along with the intestines) as bait to catch more fish.

How to Cook without Pots

Modern portable mess tins or camp cooking sets are ideal in an emergency survival situation but unless you come prepared with your own mess kit in your rucksack, you will have to improvise with whatever you can find. You might struggle to replicate Gordon Ramsay at work (except, possibly, for the swearing) but you should be able to conjure up something perfectly palatable.

How to Boil Water

Your most basic job is to boil up some water, either to sterilize it or to make a hot drink. Of course, you can't really boil water over your campfire unless you have a metal pot in which to put the water – or can you?

It may seem thoroughly implausible, but you can boil water on a campfire using a glass bottle, or even a plastic bottle. What you must do is:

1) Build a circle of small stones near your main campfire as though you were about to create a 'mini' version. Your stone circle should be larger than the base of the receptacle in which you are about to attempt to boil water.

2) Fill your glass or plastic bottle almost to the top with water. Do not put the lid on.

3) Using green sticks as tongs, or a flat stone as a shovel, transfer some embers from your main campfire into your mini fire. You need to transfer enough to keep the embers glowing hot and you can add some small dry sticks as well. Let any new

material burn down so that there are no tall flames. Embers and glowing sticks are what you want.

4) Place your receptacle upright on the embers. The water will draw the heat away from the walls of the bottle, stopping the glass from cracking or the plastic from melting, and will eventually boil.

5) Remove the bottle from the embers using two sticks as tongs or a rag as an oven glove. If you intend to drink from your bottle, wait for it to cool.

How to Fashion a Roasting Stick

Fish or meat can be roasted over a campfire using a simple roasting stick. Cut a green stick long enough for you to be able to sit at a comfortable distance from your fire so you can hold one end while the other suspends your food over the flames. You need a green stick because an older, dry stick is likely to burn through and drop your dinner into the inferno.

Sharpen one end so that you can skewer your meat or feed it through a fish from mouth to tail. Hold your food down close to the flames initially to scorch the outside and help to seal in the juices. (Perhaps Chef Ramsay will find he has some competition after all.) Your fish or meat should then be held higher so that it cooks thoroughly all the way through without burning.

If you are keen on convenience food, you can even construct a simple support on which to lean the roasting stick while you busy yourself with something else. Cut a thin branch with a 'Y' at the top, formed where the branch splits into two smaller branches. Plant this in the ground near the fire and then dig the 'handle' end of your roasting stick into the ground so that you can rest the shaft in the 'Y' of your support branch. You need to arrange all of this so that the skewer end of your roasting stick is holding the food near, or over, the fire.

How to Build a Spit Roast

While the idea of the spit roast has taken on a life of its own in the age of the superstar footballer and his WAGs, a proper chap knows that spit-roasting is something best employed in producing thrilling tucker. Really, you are simply taking the idea of a roasting stick and support one step further so that you can roast a larger item, such as a whole rabbit. You need to place a 'Y' support either side of your fire, with your food in the middle of the roasting stick, which is slotted either end into the 'Y's. Make sure that both of your supports are planted safely in the ground and that the three sticks together are strong enough to hold your dinner. If needs be, supplement the 'Y' support by lashing more sticks to each, one either side. One end of each stick should be stuck in the ground at an angle so that they cross over at the base of the 'Y'.

When cooking with a roasting-stick support or a spit roast, keep a close eye on your food to make sure that it doesn't burn. Turn it from time to time so that it cooks evenly. You don't want one side of your meat thoroughly burnt and the other side thoroughly raw.

How to Bake in a Parcel

In a variant of an old saying, you may find that you don't even have a pot to boil your vegetables in (or indeed to boil any particularly tough meat to tenderize it before roasting). Instead, you can try blanching and baking your veg.

Dig a little hollow in the ground and line it with freshly cut, large green leaves. Make sure that the leaves you are using are not poisonous. Place your vegetables in the middle of this leafy bowl and pour boiling water over them. When the water has drained away, wrap the vegetables in fresh green leaves, making little leaf parcels with the vegetables inside at least two layers of leaf, and place your leaf parcels in the embers near the edge of your campfire. How long the vegetables take to bake will depend on how hot your fire is and what kind of vegetables you are cooking. Make sure you keep the parcels surrounded by embers and unwrap a parcel to see how they are doing after an hour or so.

How to Build an Earth Oven

An alternative to baking parcels at the side of your campfire is to make a special oven. This need not take long and can produce excellent results, cooking not only vegetables but also meat or fish all at the same time.

How to Do It

1) Dig a small pit no deeper than the distance from your fingertips to your elbow. You can use the same measurement for its length and width. You should then turn one wall of the pit into a 'ramp' that leads up in the direction of the prevailing breeze.

2) Set a fire in the bottom of the pit, using plenty of kindling, tinder and larger sticks in the traditional 'wig-wam' style.

3) Lay larger dry sticks or small dry logs across the top of the pit to form a roof. Do not cover the ramp as you will need to reach down the ramp later to light your fire.

4) Balanced between the logs on the roof, place lines of stones no bigger than you can hold in one hand.

5) Add another, narrower, layer of logs on top of the stones, these logs running perpendicular to the first layer. You should now see a 'pyramid' of stones and logs starting to form.

6) Continue building until you have at least three layers of stones. Make sure that they are not porous or crumbly as these could explode when they heat up in your fire. Nor should you take stones directly from a river bed as these may be waterlogged and might also blow up when the water inside expands into steam.

7) Now light the fire in the bottom of the pit by reaching down via your ramp. Once your fire is blazing nicely, it should set light to the logs above. If it doesn't, feed more fuel in via your ramp.

8) When the log pyramid burns through, the hot stones will fall into the pit amongst the fire embers. While this is happening, you should wrap your prepared meat, fish and vegetables in large, fresh, green leaves. Leave these parcels to one side until your pyramid has collapsed.

9) Using a stick as a poker, rake the embers aside to expose the hot rocks.

10) Place your food parcels on the rocks. Meat or whatever else takes longest to cook should go to the middle of the pit.

11) Cover the whole of the bottom of the pit with green leaves and other foliage to seal in the heat, then pile on the earth that you dug out of the pit. This will keep the heat in and scavenging wildlife out. Cooking your food in an earth oven like this will take several hours – long enough for you to check your farthest snares, spot some fish for your next fishing venture, gather a fresh stock of firewood or generally explore the neighbourhood. Don't let a hungry tum tempt you to dig it all up too soon.

In the Desert

Is there a latent Lawrence of Arabia waiting to burst out of you? The desert offers challenges that only the most skilled, informed and resilient adventurer should dare to take on. For those who meet those criteria, the rewards of spending time in this singular environment are great – but the dangers omnipresent.

How to Cope with Heatstroke

If you're one of those types who has to take to a darkened, air-conditioned room at the first sign of sunshine, you hopefully won't have found your way into the desert in the first place. However, even the most hardy soul might find the heat of a sun-baked day in the Sahara too much to bear. Heatstroke is a constant danger in desert environments so take precautions to avoid it – but also know how to cope with it should it strike.

What You'll Need

Water or sports drinks
Access to shade
A hat with a wide brim all round
Baggy clothes

How to Avoid It

1) Heatstroke is caused by heat and exposure to the sun. Therefore, kick up your heels somewhere shady and cool

when the sun is at its strongest. If you have access to an air-conditioned environment, so much the better. If not, a hand-held fan is a good alternative. It may not be the most macho bit of kit, but choose one that doesn't make you look like a geisha and enjoy the benefits. Outdoor pursuits will be much cooler and more manageable in the early morning or late evening.

2) Keep hydrated. Alcohol and caffeine drinks are no good, as they will only further dehydrate you. Water is great and some sports drinks are packed with salts and minerals to replenish your stocks. Keep drinking regularly even when you don't feel thirsty. If you wait until you're gasping, you're already on the back foot. And don't drink icy cold drinks, as they can result in heat cramps in the stomach.

3) Loose-fitting clothing will, of course, keep you cooler than some body-hugging get-up. Fabrics should be thin, ventilated and preferably light coloured, as dark fabrics will absorb the sun's rays and heat you up. Any hat you wear should offer protection to your face and also to the back of your neck.

How to Treat a Casualty

If someone still falls foul of heatstroke, it is essential that you diagnose and treat quickly. If you are on your own, you will obviously need to self-treat so it is even more urgent that you realize what is happening before you are completely overcome with symptoms. You will need to make your call at the sign of the first three symptoms. Beyond that, you will have to rely on someone else.

Symptoms

1) The patient is feeling abnormally hot.
2) There is evidence of rapidly rising body temperature.
3) Patient feels drowsy.
4) Patient lapses into unconsciousness.
5) Patient starts fitting.

What to Do

1) Search out medical assistance.
2) Move the patient into the shade. Keep them calm and still, to make your job easier and to ensure they don't get any hotter.
3) Remove any clothing. Now is not the time for modesty.
4) Spray the patient with cool water and fan them to bring down the body temperature. You can also tie a piece of moistened fabric around their neck. The aim is to bring their temperature down gradually – not so suddenly that they go into shock.
5) Try to get them to take small sips of water every few minutes.
6) If ice is available, apply it around the armpits and groin.
7) If the patient has reached the stage of fitting, you must seek emergency assistance and follow some basic rules. Loosen any clothing or anything around the patient's neck. Support their head and roll them on to their side to ensure they do not choke. Tilt the head back slightly (supported with some sort of soft pillow) to keep airways open. Do not try to stop the fit – you won't succeed. But do make sure there is nothing in range on which they might hurt themselves. Do not be tempted to put anything in or around the mouth, whether

water or medicine. Ensure the patient has plenty of space and make a note of how long seizures last and any other noticeable symptoms to help the medics when they arrive. Should the patient regain consciousness, reassure them and make sure they wait for medical attention.

How to Find Water in the Desert

The biggest challenge of the desert is staying hydrated. This, as they say in common parlance, is not rocket science. So significant is the risk to you that you should haul around so much of the clear, wet stuff that the chances of running out are minimal. Otherwise, take these steps.

1) If you've not managed to load up on enough water, what chance you'll have remembered to pack a map of the local area? Well, in the small hope that you have, now is the time to make a detailed study of it in the hope of finding a symbol indicating groundwater in the surrounding area.

2) If, as I fear, the map tactic is redundant for you, take a look around your environs. Are there any forms of life, either animal or plant? If so, there must surely be water close to hand.

3) If not, your next step is to track down a dried-up river bed. Are there any signs of dampness in the nearby land? If so, it is likely that there is water just beneath surface level. Start digging. However, if no water is evident after a short while, give it up as a lost cause. There is no point exhausting yourself with digging if you find nothing to sate your thirst at the end of it.

4) If you can last out till dawn, be vigilant for early morning dew or, better still, a desert rainstorm. In the case of the latter,

have containers ready to catch some of the downpour. If there are plants nearby, check the leaves for dew. You might not find enough moisture for a morning cuppa but it will at least fend off immediate dehydration.

5) The pulp of a cactus can provide you with some essential moisture. Cut open the plant and suck the water out. In addition, make incisions into plant stems, as these sometimes prove to be stores of water.

6) Little pockets of rocks might indicate groundwater. Also, rocks in a shady area may have retained a little unevaporated rainwater.

7) Check for animal carcasses in the vicinity of a water supply. Dead animals might suggest something amiss with the water. In any case, allow water to settle in a vessel so that any silt or dirt sinks to the bottom. If you have water-purification tablets to hand, so much the better.

8) As a last resort, some experts suggest drinking your own urine may extend your chances of survival by a day or two. The inherent disadvantage in this tactic is that if you are so desperate for water, you may not be able to produce pee anyway. Besides, no less a guide than the US Field Army Manual suggests you *don't* do this as the salt content of urine will only hasten dehydration.

How to Survive a Sandstorm

A sandstorm can strike quickly and terrifyingly when a high wind sucks in sand from the desert floor, unleashing a suffocating swirl upon whatever lies before it. Here are a few tips for surviving:

1) Listen to local weather forecasts. Sandstorms can be predicted with reasonable accuracy. If you are coming into the path of one, the heroic thing to do is not to face it but to get out of the way. However, sandstorms can travel at anything up to 75 miles per hour, so don't put yourself at extra risk by speeding away from it.

2) If you've no time to escape, protect yourself as best you can. Stick tightly together with anyone else in your party. Link arms if outside. If possible, make your way to high ground where the sand is less likely to penetrate. However, if the storm is accompanied by thunder, beware of lightning and stay on lower ground.

3) If you're in a car, pull off the road, put the brake on and turn off all lights. In the confusion of a storm, tail lights have on occasion drawn other cars off the road and into the back of the illuminated vehicle. Wind up the windows and close off air vents.

4) If you are outside, try to keep your feet and legs covered, as your lower limbs are most at risk of being 'sand-blasted'.

5) Cover your nose and mouth with a damp cloth, having coated the inside of your nostrils with petroleum jelly, if at all possible. Also, put on eye protection if it's available.

6) Search out a large feature, such as a rock, as shelter. However, avoid the leeward side of a sand dune as you may end up buried in it, which would be an ironic twist to events.

In the Arctic

If you're more at home in parkier conditions, you might prefer the minimalist landscape of the Arctic. Don't be fooled into thinking that things are easier there, though. They are not, whether you are coping with the basics of keeping warm and hydrated (not as easy as you might think, considering the H_2O-heavy environment) or having to protect yourself after an unexpected accident.

How to Build a Snow Hole

If conditions suddenly take a turn for the worse while you're still a distance from base, you might decide to build a snow hole, a remarkable structure that will keep you warm despite being made from 'cold'. It is worth remembering that the build will take a good few hours, so leave yourself plenty of time and daylight.

1) You want to have a nice big, open spot for your ice palace, with lots of available snow suitable for building. The ground should be level and generally out of harm's way.

2) Pile up a great heap of snow and compact it as much as possible. A shovel really does make this stage much easier. Leave the snow for a while until it firms up with the cold, reducing the risks of a collapse mid-dig.

3) Time to start tunnelling in, creating a space a foot deep and sloping slightly upwards. It should be big enough for you to get through.

4) Now for the serious excavation work as you dig out a domed

cell within the snow big enough for you and whoever you will be sharing the night with. It needs to be able to cope with your bulk lying down and sitting up. If the roof drips, smooth it off.

5) Drill an air hole in the roof and make sure it extends all the way through to the air above. The snow above your head should be at least 2 feet (60cm) thick. Do not miss this stage out or your lovely, comfy night in the snow hole may prove to be your last.

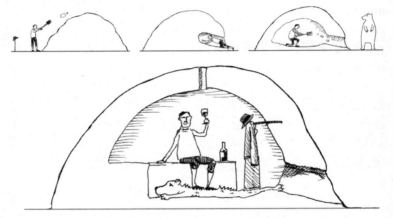

6) Let your architectural flair go wild within the cell. You can sculpt seating, sleeping alcoves, indeed whatever your imagination can conjure up. The higher up you are when at rest, the warmer you will be. Cover the ground for insulation.

7) Invite in all the inhabitants. Close off the entrance with, say, your backpack to keep out the cold.

8) Prepare for a cosy night in.

How to Get Water from Snow and Ice

Even the least observant among us will soon notice that the Arctic is predominantly snow and ice. And even those who failed to pay proper attention during First Year science will know that snow and ice are made of water. So you have no excuse for getting thirsty. Nonetheless, there are some factors to bear in mind.

Do not simply suck a block of ice or eat fistfuls of snow – you will only manage to dehydrate yourself further as your mouth and belly struggle to melt it. You must always pre-melt instead, capturing the water in a suitable vessel. And don't wait for crisis point before stocking up on water. Harvesting snow or ice can be tiring and uses up precious energy.

Snow, of course, falls from the sky and so it will be as clean as rainwater. This means that it might contain all sorts of dubious chemicals inherited along the way but you won't have to worry about micro-organisms (apart from those it might have picked up while lying around. When people say 'never eat yellow snow', they really do have a point!).

Ice, on the other hand, might consist of fresh or salt water. A general rule of thumb is that ice with a bluish tinge is pure and ice with a greyish tinge is salty. Salt ice can be desalinated but it is an extra complication best avoided if possible. 'Pure' ice is generally preferable to snow as you will need a greater volume of snow to produce an equal amount of water and because snow is a less efficient conductor of heat, meaning you will need more energy to melt it.

Melting is best done using a pan and stove. Preferably, the pan should contain a little water to help with heat conduction.

Smaller chunks of ice will melt quicker than large pieces so break up bigger lumps (while being careful not to injure yourself with flying fragments).

As a rough rule of thumb, you will need twice the amount of fuel to *melt* the ice in freezing conditions as you would need to *boil* the same volume of water on an average summer's day. You'll then need half the energy again to boil the melted water. Boiling is advisable to help purify the water, but you should also strain it and use chemical purifiers if at all possible.

If you need to melt snow/ice without the aid of a stove, there are a few alternatives. In each case, you must have a suitable vessel to catch the water as it melts. You can simply compact handfuls of snow on the end of a stick and spear the stick into the ground, close to a heat source such as a fire, and wait for nature to take its course. Or, rather than making a 'snow stick', you could fill a bag with snow and ice, and wait for that to melt over a receptacle. This has the added advantage of filtering out some larger contaminants through the fabric of the bag. In the absence of fire, any dark material that absorbs solar heat can be used as a heat source.

As a last resort, you can use your own body heat. As long as you are healthy and have ample provisions, you won't be risking too much energy of your own, although it will be a rather uncomfortable experience and can take many hours.

How to Escape from Ice

You know how thick and strong the ice can be in the Arctic. You have seen how it can easily support the weight of a great polar bear in those adverts for mints from years ago. So surely you won't have a problem, even if you have sensibly upped your fatty deposits and are wearing goodness knows how many extra layers of clothes. Then all of a sudden . . . ahhh . . . you're through the ice and flailing around in freezing cold water. What should you do?

1) The body will naturally respond to the shock of falling through ice. You are likely to have the puff knocked out of you and your body will start to curl up as it goes on the defensive. However, you must make sure that you get your breathing under control, fill your lungs full of air, and get full control over your limbs.

2) You have just fallen through the ice so you can reasonably assume that it is not as strong as you might expect just around there. If you put all your weight on one or two areas (perhaps as you try to pull yourself free using your hands or elbows), you might succeed only in causing more ice to break. This is energy-sapping and leaves you in a bigger hole. Instead, stretch your arms out flat on the ice, thus distributing your weight, and while keeping flat attempt to roll out of the icy water.

3) If you succeed, do not spring to your feet and start punching the air with joy and dancing a jig of thanks. Instead stay flat to the ice and slowly drag yourself to safety, all the time spreading your weight over as big an area as possible.

4) If this doesn't work, you are going to have to rely on getting assistance. Shout loudly, but stay calm. You will be OK for a good 15–20 minutes so don't fly into a panic. And when help arrives, warn your rescuers to keep their weight spread as they approach you. Another man through the ice will be no help at all.

5) Once you are freed, you will clearly need to get fresh,

dry clothes on as soon as possible and start to bring your body temperature back up. You may well have become as dehydrated as if you had survived a calamity in a much hotter climate, so be sure to replenish your fluids too.

Up in the Air

To fly is to enjoy man's ability to master even the seemingly impossible – to travel through the air inside a big metal bird. However, when things go wrong up there, you have real problems. No situation is hopeless, though, so here is how to make the best of even the most desperate scenario.

How to Land a Small Aircraft When the Pilot is Incapacitated

We all love those wonderful men in their flying machines. But what if you find yourself the passenger in a light aircraft when that 'wonderful man' takes the opportunity to keel over? A heart attack? A dodgy curry the night before? A sudden case of vertigo? Who cares? What you really need to know is how to get back to terra firma in full working order.

How You'll Survive

1) First things first, stay calm. Panic may seem an attractive strategy in the moment but it's the surest way to disaster. Think rationally. A good many aircraft these days have an autopilot system which, once set and engaged, will steer the plane on a pre-decided route. And even if there is no autopilot, the pilot will have 'trimmed' the aircraft so that he could pilot it 'hands off'. That is to say, the plane will keep going at a constant speed and height along a selected course. The 'belt-and-braces' approach to flying will also have seen

your pilot file a full flight plan with the local air-traffic control (ATC) so that they can keep track of you.

2) Now, make sure the pilot's feet are safely away from the rudder pedals, which are roughly where the pedals are in a motor car. Ensure that his hands and body are not obstructing the control column (also known as the 'yoke' or 'joystick'). With a bit of luck, there will be dual controls in your plane, so you can simply slip into the co-pilot's seat next to the pilot. If there is only one set, you will have to move the pilot and assume his seat.

3) Once in situ, compose yourself and don't start grasping madly for the controls. You wouldn't have liked it if the pilot had done that, so don't do it yourself. Survey the instrument panel in front of you and try to find the attitude indicator (also called an 'artificial horizon'  or 'gyro horizon'). It will probably be in the middle of the top row. It will show you the position of the aircraft in relation to the ground. You will be able to see if the wings are level, if you are climbing, descending or going along at a constant height. The dial will show a sphere divided crossways, with the blue upper half representing the sky and the brown lower half the earth. The pair of straight lines you'll see are your wings and the white dot between is the plane's nose.

4) If the wings and nose do not line up with the red 'horizon'

on the dial, you may assume the autopilot is off. In this case you will need to get the plane on a level. The joystick is an extremely sensitive bit of equipment so you will need to treat it gently to achieve this. Pull it back and you will raise the nose; push it forward and the nose comes down. Move it to the left and the plane banks left; to the right it will bank right. Carefully adjust appropriately until your wings on the attitude indicator line up with the horizon. You will not need to employ the rudder pedals at all.

5) You now need to identify the radio, probably to be found in the centre of the instrument panel. If there is no obvious microphone, put on the pilot's headset, find and operate the PTT (Press to Talk) button and repeat the word 'Mayday' three times in a cool, calm and collected manner. Then say 'Pilot unconscious' and release the PTT button so that whoever receives the message can respond to you.

6) Underneath the radio is the transponder, which allows ATC to track your position on radar. Either type in or set the dials to '7700', the code for 'general emergency' that will alert ATC. (Note, you are already becoming familiar with a wealth of acronyms, an essential part of being a real pilot.)

7) Once an ATC operator is on the case, you are flying (both literally and metaphorically). The secret of flying is to be in control of four factors: height, speed, course and attitude (the angle of the aircraft relative to the ground). Listen to the controller's step-by-step instructions, following them precisely and asking for repetition or clarification whenever necessary. The controller will talk you through so that you get the aircraft down to a height from which you can safely

land. He will explain how to control the engine power, lower the undercarriage (though many light aircraft have a fixed undercarriage) and turn on to a new course. He will guide you round the various relevant instruments, including the altimeter (which measures the aircraft's height above the ground) and the airspeed indicator.

8) It may be unrealistic to get you to fly back to an aerodrome, so you might have to land in a field or even on a road. Stay alert for any obstacles including trees, power lines, buildings or bridges. Keep the controller apprised of anything that might be a problem.

9) Approach your landing place in a straight line. As you are about to touch the ground, pull back the joystick so that the nose rises and you land on the main wheels under the wings. As you slow down, the nose wheel will come down.

10) As soon as the main wheels touch earth, pull back the throttle (a big black lever located between the pilot and co-pilot seats, or else a large knob – usually black – in the middle at the bottom of the instrument panel). Some light aircraft also have toe brakes on the rudder pedals; press them gently to bring the plane to a stop without skidding.

11) There may be a key, like the ignition key of a car, on the instrument panel. Once you have come to a full stop, turn it to shut off the engine. Give the ailing pilot whatever help you can. Do not attempt to disembark from the plane until the propeller has stopped turning.

How to Survive if Your Parachute Doesn't Open

To leap out of an aircraft thousands of feet up, pull the cord to open your parachute and find it doesn't work might well be the definition of 'a pickle'. You will have precious time to think and will need to rely on your survival instincts kicking in. Whatever the outcome, it will most certainly hurt. The question is, will you live to see another day? Well, you just might if you can find a friend.

What to Do

1) As soon as you know there is a problem, indicate as such to a colleague who has yet to open their own chute. You should do this by waving your arms and pointing at your chute.

2) Your fellow jumper will hopefully move over towards you. When you are face to face, you must lock arms. And remember to add them to your Christmas card list.

3) Now you must hook your arms up to your elbows into your partner's chest strap or, alternatively, through both sides of the front of his harness. Then grab hold of your own strap.

4) By now, you and your chum will be hurtling through the sky at what is disconcertingly called terminal velocity (roughly 130 miles per hour), with all sorts of unpleasant forces wreaking mayhem on your combined weights.

5) When your colleague's chute now opens, you will experience a massive shock which will most likely break your arms or pop them out of their sockets. I did mention that it would hurt.

6) Your partner must keep hold of you with one hand while using the other to steer the canopy. If his chute is big, your descent will hopefully be slow enough that you get away with just a broken leg. If it's a small canopy, he'll have to steer hard to slow things down. If there is a body of water nearby, he should make for that and you should get ready to tread water. You'll have to rely on him to get you to safety before your chute takes on water and takes you under, but he will have seen you right so far so have faith.

Needless to say, your best bet is to make sure your chute is in good working order and perfectly packed before you get anywhere near an aircraft.

In the Water

Around water is no place for horseplay. Even on the calmest of days, accidents can happen. By far and away the majority of people who drown are fully clothed – only 20 per cent of drowning victims meet their fate wearing swimming costumes. Anyone who falls overboard from a boat while on a pleasure or fishing trip, or slips and falls from a quayside or rocks, is likely to do so while fully clothed and wearing shoes, making life very difficult for even the strongest swimmers. Should you ever find yourself in this position, stay calm and use this 'drown-proofing' technique as you gather some strength.

How to Save a Drowning Swimmer

1) Get your head above water and take a deep breath.
2) Close your mouth, hold your breath and lower your face into the water.
3) Stretch your arms out in front of you on the surface of the water.
4) Your legs will now start to drift towards the surface behind you. They will not make it all the way to the surface.
5) Relax in this position. The air in your lungs will be an aid to buoyancy, keeping you stable in this 'dead man's float' position.
6) When you are ready for another breath, probably after ten seconds or so, slowly raise your arms. Your legs will now separate slightly and drift downwards.
7) Raise your head high enough to get your mouth out of the

water, exhale, take another deep breath and resume the 'dead man's float'.

You will not be able to repeat this procedure indefinitely, but it does give you the opportunity to rest should you need it. This can be very important if you are in the water with a rescued swimmer for whom you have managed to secure an effective float. If you are both stranded in the water, you might need to rest so that you can carry on helping.

However, it would be better to have avoided this situation in the first place. Getting into the water with a swimmer in distress is something to do only when you have dismissed all other alternatives. In an adventure movie, the hero will rip off his shirt, kick off his shoes and dive into the water. But this is not *Baywatch*. Use your head and you will be taking the first step towards rescuing the swimmer in trouble. Before even entering the water, work through the following steps:

1) Observe. Is this person really in trouble or just horsing around with friends?

2) Think fast. A panicking adult in trouble in the water may drown in only one minute. A child will not take that long.

3) Assess the risks. You need to judge the nature of the water with which you will be dealing. Is it a fast-flowing river? Is there an undertow on the beach? Is the swimmer caught in an overpowering current?

4) Shout for help. If you need to get into the water, someone else can call the emergency services.

5) Look for a way to reach the swimmer. Observe the golden rules: Reach to Him, Throw to Him, Paddle to Him, Swim to Him.

6) Reach to Him. Use a tree branch or any kind of pole, perhaps a fishing rod, to reach out towards the swimmer, yelling at him to grab hold. You can also use an item of clothing. Holding on to one sleeve of a shirt or jacket, the other sleeve will reach out quite far over the water. If you can reach to him with your hand, you must avoid being pulled into the water. Lie flat on the ground with your legs spread to give you the best balance. Only reach out with one arm, keeping the other on dry land. Make sure that you do not let your shoulders slip out over the water.

7) Throw to Him. Is there a life ring nearby? Otherwise, throw anything that will float to the swimmer – a beach ball, an air mattress or a wave board. With a float to cling on to, he will be able to keep his head above water, catch his breath and start to calm down. Throw him a rope, if you can find one quickly, and tow him to dry land.

8) Paddle to Him. Any kind of boat becomes a lifeboat in an emergency, from a pedalo or a kayak to a dinghy or punt. Be careful when approaching the swimmer, especially in rough seas or a strong current. If a wave suddenly rocks the boat and it hits your swimmer on the head, he could be knocked

unconscious, making the situation immeasurably worse. Rather than rowing close to the swimmer, encourage him to come to you, then throw him a lifeline of some kind. If you are in a small boat, it is safer for him to cling on to something and be towed ashore rather than risk capsizing the boat as you try to haul him aboard.

9) Swim to Him – but only if wading is not an option. You should be stable in the water until it gets as deep as your groin. If you can wade close to him, you may be able to reach him with a lifeline or branch. You should also carry with you a stick as tall as your shoulder to give yourself support and to probe ahead to make sure that your next footstep will not take you under. When you are close enough, reach out to the swimmer with your stick or an item of clothing so that you can tow him in. Don't let him grab hold of you as he may drag you under the water. Keep your distance by towing him, then help him out once you have reached the water's edge before climbing out yourself.

If you must swim, do not go right up to him. Keep out of his reach and throw him a lifeline so that you can tow him to safety. If you get close enough for a panicking person who is in fear for his life to grab hold of you, he may try to climb on top of you to keep himself out of the water. Should this happen you must free yourself from his grip and swim out of his range. Calm him down and tell him to stop thrashing around, to tilt his head back and spread his arms out so that he will float. Once he is in this position, you can approach him from behind, where it will be more difficult for him to grab you should he start to panic again.

Keep talking to him, explaining what you are about to do and telling him that you will have him safe and sound on dry land in no time. The more confident and reassuring you sound, the more likely he is to remain calm.

There are a number of different techniques that can be used to help the victim to safety, but in a work of this length is it not possible to go into them in detail. They are best learned and perfected by attending a professionally run lifesaving course, such as those officially approved by the Royal Lifesaving Society UK (http://www.lifesavers.org.uk/courses.html).

If you think that you are going to be in the water for a while, you will find swimming easier, especially when towing your rescued swimmer, if you can shed some clothing, although if the water is cold, even wet clothes will help you to retain some body warmth. A waterproof, such as an anorak, can also be used to make a temporary float. By knotting the sleeves and waving it with a scooping motion over your head, you should be able to scrunch up the open ends of the sleeves, trapping enough air inside for them to balloon out. Your float will lose its air after a while, but it could give you a couple of minutes to catch your breath and recover some strength.

How to Deal with a Capsized Sailboat

There you are cruising around on a sailboat, secretly pretending you're a young Simon le Bon in the video for 'Rio'. Then suddenly things go wrong and you feel the boat capsizing. As ever, the first thing you must do is keep yourself calm. Hopefully you will have prepared ahead of your trip. This is the time when a bag of emergency supplies really comes into its own. Also, leave a copy of your itinerary on land with someone you trust and who will notice when you haven't come back. And always, always wear a life jacket. So Simon le Bon didn't in the 'Rio' video, but it might just save your bacon. But what should you do if your boat capsizes and throws you into the water?

1) If there are others with you, check for anybody struggling in the water. Give them whatever assistance you can but under no circumstances make a grab for them. This is likely to induce panic and make tragedy more likely (see pages 84–5.)

2) Once the mast is in the water, untie all the sheets (ropes) controlling the sails. This means that, should the boat right itself, it won't then sail off into the distance without you.

3) Try to get to the bottom of the boat, locate the centreboard and stand on it. With a bit of luck, this will right the boat. Point the boat into the wind, climb back in, gather yourself and make your way to safety.

4) If that doesn't work, you will have to go to Plan B. By and large, your boat will be more efficient at floating than you. Stay with it and try to climb on to its upturned hull. It will be easier for the emergency services to find you and you should be warmer than in the water.

5) If you were carrying a mobile phone, see if you still have it and how it has fared in the water. Call for help if at all possible.

6) If you have fresh water, keep drinking a little regularly. Dehydration is a major threat in a capsize incident. Also, try to keep yourself shaded, even if just under a hat or one improvised from a T-shirt. Do not drink seawater, which will only dehydrate you.

7) If you spot a plane or another boat approaching, you need to get their attention. Are there any flares to hand? If not, can you find a small mirror or something similar to reflect the sun's light?

8) If you are a strong swimmer and close to land, you might decide to make a bid for freedom. But beware, landmarks may seem very much closer than they are in the middle of a large water mass. Don't begin a paddle that you can't finish. Much better to stay near the relative safety of the boat and await rescue.

How to Make a Raft

You're on an adventure and you decide that you need to travel on the river rather than on foot. Perhaps you have a cargo to carry, or an injured colleague to transport. Or perhaps you just fancy a change of scene. You could spend days or weeks crafting yourself a truly wonderful canoe or you could save the time and dedicate just a few hours to build yourself a raft. If done properly, a raft is a wonderfully simple and effective bit of engineering that is bound to bring you satisfaction as you consider what an effective team you and nature make.

What You'll Need

A knife
Some rope
Logs
(and maybe a saw)

How to Do It

1) First, you need your basic material – logs. If you're lucky, you will find a supply of felled logs, all of just the right shape and size. More likely, you will need to cut your own (having made sure it is legal to do so). Search out some young, mid-sized trees. It may well be that you didn't bring your entire shed of tools when you embarked on your trip, but hopefully you will have packed a lightweight wire saw in your kit. If you didn't, you may look forward to continuing your journey on dry land only.

2) Decide how big you want your raft to be. Six feet by six feet should be ample for a one-man craft. You will need enough logs for the four sides of the frame and for the 'decking'.

3) Start your build close to the water's edge. You won't want to have to lug your handiwork further than necessary to launch it.

4) Take four of the logs and saw out a section a few inches deep along their lengths.

5) Place two of these 'notched' logs parallel to each other just short of a log's length apart. Set the other 'notched logs' to one side.

6) With two more 'un-notched' logs, form a square with overlapping corners. Lash the corners with your rope, beginning with a clove hitch and finishing with an overhand knot on each corner.

clove hitch → 〈 〉 ← overhand knot

← half hitch

7) You are now ready to lay the decking, lashing each new log to the frame before tying with a half hitch. Your logs should all be of comparable size but make sure any larger ones are evenly distributed.

8) Once all the decking is in place, position the last two

'notched' logs over the ends of the decking logs. Lash the corners as before, and add further lashing along the mid-sections.

9) Find a long branch to steer your vessel.

10) Enjoy your new role as Admiral of the Fleet.

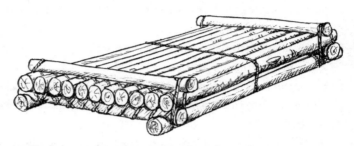

How to Cross a Swollen River

No one in their right mind would ever choose to wade across a swollen river but under emergency circumstances you may have no choice. Only a life-threatening emergency will make it worthwhile though. If you spot an injured person who needs urgent assistance on the far bank, then fair enough – but take the greatest care. You are no good to anyone if you become another casualty. On the other hand, if you're thinking of diving in to retrieve a mis-kicked football, consider whether that bit of inflated leather is worth risking your life.

In the event that you decide there is no choice but to attempt a crossing, remember that however strong and steady on your feet you may think you are, a fast-flowing body of water (or a fast-flowing area in a body of water) that barely reaches your knees can easily be powerful enough to sweep you off your feet. Disoriented, perhaps having sucked in a lungful of water or bumped your head, you can then find yourself being swept away downstream. So take some steps to ensure your safety before entering the water.

1) Evaluate the risk and study the stretch of water you are about to cross. This need not take long. Does it look like the water gets significantly deeper towards the middle? If the water is clear, throw in a few stones and watch how they settle at various points to help you judge the depth. You will be taking a grave risk trying to wade through moving water that is more than waist deep. Any more than waist deep and you will almost certainly have to swim. Also, check the water temperature. Even in the height of summer, water coming down off a mountain can be bitterly cold – cold enough, in fact, to give you quite a shock and send your muscles into cramp: something you need to prepare for mentally.

2) Can you see leaves, twigs, branches or other debris in the water? Are these moving faster at some points than others? Is there enough debris in the water to cause danger to you should it hit you as you are crossing? If there is none in the water, try throwing some in, like some twigs, to land at various points across the water. This could be the game of 'Pooh Sticks' that saves your life.

3) The narrowest part of a river may not be the best place to try to cross. A wider stretch may be shallower, with the water flowing more slowly. Take some time to investigate up and downstream to find a suitable point. Is there an island in a stream that looks tempting as a halfway rest spot? Consider whether you will be able to drag yourself out of the water on to an island, or whether, in fact, it turns one wide, shallow river

into two faster flowing, deeper rivers. In splitting the flow of water, there may also be more turbulence downstream from an island, making it more dangerous there than upstream.

4) Nor is a bend in the river the best place to cross. The current is likely to be stronger on the outside of the bend than it is on the inside. And can you see 'stepping stones' that look like they could get you across? Rocks that are flat and dry might work well for you, but never be tempted to try leaping from boulder to boulder to try to cross a river without getting your feet wet. You can easily lose your footing on slippery wet rocks and end up in the water, perhaps with a sprained ankle or a broken limb, maybe even unconscious.

5) Having chosen your crossing point, find or cut yourself a stout staff as straight and thick as a walking stick and long enough to reach up to your shoulder.

6) Before you get into the water, take off your boots, socks and trousers, then put your boots back on. Don't worry, you're not at a fashion parade. You will need your boots for grip and to protect your feet from any sharp rocks, tree roots or other objects that you may not be able to see on the river bed. If you don't have a plastic bag to keep them dry in your rucksack, put your socks in your trouser pockets and tie your trousers around your neck. When you have finished your crossing, you will be far warmer and more comfortable if your socks and trousers are dry.

7) Getting into and out of the water can be awkward if you can't find a gentle incline down which to walk into the river. If you have to step in off a low riverbank, use your staff to probe the river bed first to make sure that you will not sink

into mud and to locate any submerged obstacles.

8)   Do not rush. Move forwards only as quickly as you feel it is safe to do so. Use your staff to probe in front of you and then step forward to where you feel you will have secure footing. As you move ahead, plant your staff firmly on the river bed at a slight angle on the downstream side of your body so that it can act as a support should you be hit by floating debris or a strong current.

9)   Once you have stepped forward a pace or two, probe ahead with the staff again, looking for hidden dangers such as sudden deep water and stronger currents. Hold the staff ready to use as a support again while you step forward once more.

10) When you reach the other side, plant your staff downstream to act as a support if you need to climb out.

How to Escape from Quicksand

Finding yourself in this natural anomaly is to experience solid earth behaving more like liquid glue. A staple of many a horror film, getting trapped does not necessarily signal the end.

Where to Expect Quicksand

Quicksand forms where water has saturated the soil or sand, lubricating the sand particles to such an extent that the friction of the rough surface of one particle against another will no longer bind them together. You can expect to find quicksand:

• Near the seashore
• On a riverbank

- Around the edge of a lake
- In bogs or marshland
- In an area where the soil type changes or there are underground streams
- On any wet ground during an earthquake. Because an earthquake causes the soil to vibrate, it can loosen the hold that the soil particles have on each other and, in wet ground, water will flood in between them. An earthquake can, therefore, turn what was a perfectly normal patch of solid ground into quicksand where there was none before.

What Happens When You Walk on Quicksand?

Quicksand can look like a marshy piece of land or a patch of wet sand. Unhelpfully, it may also look like perfectly ordinary sand or soil because of the way that the water circulates below the surface. A thin crust of air-dried sand can be sitting on the surface and leaves and twigs will settle on top of the quicksand without sinking. You might not be able to see any movement in this liquid soil and you could think that you are walking forward over perfectly solid ground.

However, you will soon be able to tell if you're walking on quicksand on account of you sinking. It does not feel like stepping into a swimming pool and going straight to the bottom. The sand has certain liquid properties, but it is a viscous liquid, something more akin to treacle. And that is where its real danger lies.

The first thing that happens when you jump in a normal swimming pool is that, whether you reach the bottom or not, once you stop falling through the water, you start to come back to the surface. This is because the density of water is greater than that of the human body – so we float. Treacle, of course, is more dense than water, so you would float in treacle, too. Technically, then, you will float on the surface of quicksand. Alas, the pressure of having all of your weight on the small area of the sole of one foot as you step forward forces that foot down through the quicksand in the same way you would expect your foot to be forced down through water.

With no solid ground to push up against, you have the additional challenge of waterlogged soil above your foot. A swift upward movement will remove your foot from the soil that was compacting below it, creating a gap. A vacuum, which, as we all know, nature abhors and must immediately fill, sucking in whatever is nearby. More quicksand will be sucked in to fill the gap below your foot and the gap will be trying to suck in your foot, too.

Multiply the effect just described acting on one foot to accommodate the other foot, knees, thighs, hands and elbows and you can see how someone can start to feel like quicksand is swallowing them up.

How to Extricate Yourself

Your first reactions when you feel yourself sinking into what you thought was dry land may well be surprise and panic. Panic, of course, tends to lead to frenzied movement and, as we have seen, this will make things worse. If you find yourself in quicksand, therefore, the most effective way to get yourself out is as follows:

1) Stay calm and try not to make sudden or erratic movements. If you fall over, you'll be in real straits.

2) Spread your legs and, if necessary, your arms to distribute your weight over a larger area.

3) Lean at an angle, preferably towards the nearest bit of solid ground. This presents a larger surface area to the quicksand and helps to slow the rate at which you sink.

4) Using only small, slow movements, stabilize yourself in the quicksand. You will be able to float on your back on the surface of the quicksand.

5) Make gentle rowing motions with your arms across the surface to paddle slowly towards dry land.

6) If you have a long staff with you (you did prepare properly for your walk, didn't you?), it will help your buoyancy to have this stick underneath you, across your body.

On the Road

The modern driving experience – one of tailbacks, speed humps and road rage – is, sadly, far removed from the grand traditions of motoring. In days gone by, ownership of a car allowed an escape from the pressures of everyday life and a chance to swap the mundane for the spectacular and/or relaxing. The automobile, it must be remembered, is a beast of burden under the lordship of its driver. Too often, today, we seem to be in thrall to our vehicles. That is not the attitude; it is you who must be in control. Occasionally the road will throw up a situation that sends shock waves through you and it is then that you must be ready to seize the initiative. Here are some, thankfully reasonably uncommon, scenarios and strategies for dealing with them.

How to Escape from a Car in Water

There are few things more frightening than to go off the road in a vehicle and find yourself submerged under water. That said, you stand a reasonable chance of surviving but only if you keep your panic levels under control and know what to do. Firstly, you should adopt the brace position to cushion you from the impact of hitting the water. Put each hand on the opposite side of your head so that your arms are crossed. With your outside hand, get a hold of the seat belt. If your car is floating, attempt your escape before it starts to fill up. But if you're already going under (and in particularly deep water, the car may also overturn), you will need to work through the following steps:

1) Open your window as quickly as possible. Yes, it will feel counter-intuitive but, unless you have managed to open your car door in the microseconds before it went below the water level, it is the only way to equalize the pressure inside and outside the car quickly enough. Without that equalization, your door won't open. If the car's built-in window-opening system doesn't work, use your feet, shoulder or something heavy to hand to smash the glass. Focus on the side and rear windows rather than the toughened windshield. Keep your fellow passengers (especially any children) calm and explain to them what they will need to do while the car fills. Once the water level has got up to chest height, take a final deep breath and hold your nose. You might also try to turn on any lights, which might help you to focus and will also serve as a signal to a rescue party.

2) Put your hand on the door latch. Do this early, before the ingress of water obscures your vision. It is worth keeping your seat belt on while the car fills with water so that the

incoming water does not fling you out of position.

3) As soon as you can, unlock the door(s). It is inevitable that you will be feeling stressed but take slow, deep breaths for as long as there is air in the car and approach your work as calmly as possible. Escape through the door. If you have been unable to open it, you can exit through the window if it is big enough. This will use up valuable time and energy though.

4) You should help to release the belts of any other passengers in need of assistance, before pushing them out of the car with you following. On emerging into the outside water, don't be tempted to kick your feet if there is a chance of striking fellow passengers.

5) You must, naturally, get to the surface as quickly as you can. Use the car as a 'springboard' upwards. If you are disorientated and don't know which way is up, look for any lights or streams of bubbles (which always rise), or allow yourself to float for a couple of seconds.

6) Once you have emerged from the water, seek out medical assistance even if you think you're unscathed.

How to Cope with Skidding on Ice

Anyone who has tentatively stepped on to an ice-skating rink will know how much more difficult it is to move in a controlled manner when you have no grip between your feet and the ground beneath. It is no easier to drive a car on snow or ice when maintaining traction is virtually impossible. If your wheels cannot grip the road surface, you will not be able to steer properly, the wheels driven by the engine (whether you have front-wheel, rear-wheel or four-wheel drive) will spin, your brakes will not work and your vehicle will skid. There are certain drivers, who can be generically labelled as *Homo pratticus*, who believe that forcing their cars into skidding somehow demonstrates their skill at the wheel. The truth is that you have lost control once you go into a skid – skidding causes 48 per cent of the accidents on Britain's roads in winter. The skill is to extract your vehicle from its slide and reassert your authority.

To stand any chance, you need to make sure your tyres are fit for the road at all times. In some countries it is mandatory to fit winter tyres from November through to April. Winter tyres are 'chunkier' than normal road tyres with wider water channels and softer rubber to give better grip. For winter sports enthusiasts, when driving into the mountains to reach a ski resort, it may be compulsory to fit snow chains. Most modern types of snow chain are simple to fit in just a few minutes and in areas where they are likely to be required, a fitting service is often available at service stations. However, they must be removed when driving on clear roads as they damage the road surface.

Normally, though, road tyres in good condition and correctly inflated are generally perfectly adequate for winter use, providing that you observe proper precautions when driving on snow or ice. There are a few simple rules to follow:

1) Reduce your speed.
2) Avoid aggressive acceleration, which can cause your wheels to spin.
3) Avoid harsh braking, which can cause your wheels to lock and your tyres to lose their traction.
4) Avoid violent steering.

If you do find yourself in a skid, recovering control depends on a number of factors, including whether you have front-wheel, rear-wheel or four-wheel drive; the nature of the skid and the road conditions. Generally speaking, you should point the front wheels in the direction you want the vehicle to go, keep your foot off the brake and put the car in neutral until you have slowed enough to regain control.

Maintaining traction on your drive wheels is often simply a case of having enough weight over the wheels. Under normal weather conditions, carrying a heavy load will increase your fuel consumption but in winter, if you have a rear-wheel drive car, carrying a bag of sand in the boot can help your tyres to grip. Front-wheel drive cars have the engine over the drive wheels to aid traction but when trying to negotiate a steep incline, the weight will be thrown to the back. To stop your front wheels from spinning under these conditions, and if it is safe to do so, you can try reversing up the slope.

How to Deal with a Stuck Accelerator and Failing Brakes

Modern cars are blessed with remarkably efficient braking systems but in recent times there have been notable instances of major car manufacturers recalling models because they suspect a problem. But what if you're doing 70mph on the motorway before the problem kicks in? The car ahead is stopping so you take your foot off the gas but nothing happens. As the tagline goes for that famous film about a bus that will not slow down, 'What do you do? What do you do?' As ever, your immediate response must be: 'I will not panic.'

How to Cope with a Jammed Accelerator

A nightmare scenario with a reasonably straightforward solution. While your first response will be to want to un-jam the accelerator, you should instead turn your focus towards the brake and clutch; that is to say, the things that are working properly.

1) Firmly depress the foot brake to override the accelerator. Gently pump the brake if you need to. Do not be tempted to employ the handbrake, as the chances are you'll burn out your brake pads and very possibly send yourself into a spin.

2) Depress the clutch. This has the effect of preventing the engine from powering the car. If you're in an automatic, put the gear in neutral instead.

3) As you continue to brake, search for a viable escape route, such as on to the hard shoulder. You might be tempted to get on to it as soon as possible but you should steer over gently and calmly. You're in a fast-moving vehicle and any erratic driving will only destabilize you further. With a bit of luck, you should have slowed the car down within ten seconds, averting disaster.

4) If the clutch is not working, only then consider turning off the engine.

How to Cope with Non-Responsive Brakes

As you can see, the above scenario may be simply resolved. But what if the brakes let you down too? Well, first off, that is not very likely, especially in modern vehicles with dual brakes. But if they do, you can turn once again to the clutch. As before, the clutch should always be your first port of call ahead of cutting out the engine with your ignition keys. Use the clutch and work down gradually through the gears. If this proves problematic at high speeds, you might want to apply your handbrake very delicately.

And if the clutch has gone as well? Once you have got through all this, you may want to think back to any black cats who crossed your path or lucky-heather sellers that you inadvertently offended. In the meantime, you will need to turn off your ignition. However, be sure to leave the key in situ. If you attempt to take it out, the steering will lock and you'll be in a whole new realm of trouble.

If the key has somehow stuck as well, things start to look even bleaker. A phone call to the emergency services would be a start if you can do so safely, and then you will probably want to seek out as safe a route as possible. Up a grass verge or on to the gravel of an HGV escape lane would be recommended, although you are still probably going to get hurt. Away from the motorway, there is little you can do but aim to avoid causing damage to others and brace yourself for what lies ahead. Sideswiping trees, bushes or even vehicles (preferably uninhabited) can all help to slow you down, as can steering sharply from side-to-side. You can also engage aerodynamics to lessen your pace by opening windows and (if practical) the doors too. Ultimately, you need to identify as soft a spot as possible to crash, where no one else is going to be at risk. Good luck!

How to Cope with a Tyre Blow-Out

You're cruising along the road, carefree and listening to that CD of questionable 70s prog-rock that you were given last Father's Day, when suddenly the car feels like it's taken on a life of its own. After a moment or two of rising panic, you realize that one of the tyres has blown out. If you're going to keep your motor under control and its inhabitants unharmed, you must take a deep breath and wrestle back control.

1) Your first step to getting a grip of the situation is to get a grip of the steering wheel. Make sure you have both hands firmly on it and maintain a straight course. Gradually take your foot off the accelerator to reduce your speed.

2) Slowly depress the brake. While you want the car to slow, any sudden braking is more likely to make you lose control

of the vehicle.

3) Having indicated, make for the hard shoulder or side of the road, steering smoothly. Get as far away from moving traffic as you safely can.

4) Having parked up the car, put on your hazard lights and lay out your warning triangle if you have one. Do not put yourself in danger by straying too close to oncoming traffic.

The modern motorist has the luxury of being able to call on any one of several emergency roadside services, who will be able to tow you off to somewhere suitable to sort out your car's predicament. However, it is well worth being versed in the art of the wheel change so that you can sort the problem out yourself.

In fact, if you aren't, you shouldn't be driving, not least because the adventurous chap will always be ready and willing to assist a member of the gentler sex who may not have that skill (although many do), or who may lack the strength required.

How to Escape a Road Ambush

You don't necessarily have to be an SAS operative to find yourself in the middle of an armed ambush on the road. It is, regretfully, a hazard that you might encounter in many spots throughout the world. Where you see an averagely remunerated middle manager

in the mirror, others may see their chance of a life-altering ransom demand. There can be few things more terrifying than seeing the road ahead blocked by a hostile vehicle and while the guidelines below won't turn you into a proto-Jack Bauer, they will give you some strategies when you might otherwise feel utterly vulnerable.

1) Do not freeze. This will be your natural instinct but it won't help you at all. You need to take in the scenario ahead of you, choose a course of action and execute it as rapidly as possible.

2) Why are you under attack? Are your assailants likely to be seeking only your death? In that situation, evasive action is the only answer. But if you think you are the subject of a kidnap-for-ransom (where you are worth more to your attackers alive than dead), and if your chances of escaping them are slim, surrendering yourself might be the preferred option.

3) If you decide you need to escape (and perhaps there are bullets already flying at you), you need to prepare for impact. Get down as low as possible (and tell your passengers to do the same), put your lights on full beam, have a look in your mirrors to see if you're also being attacked from behind, grip the steering wheel with the edge of your thumbs (to keep as much out of harm's way as possible) and prepare for a shattered windscreen.

4) You must now make the decision either to try and break through the ambush or reverse out of the situation.

How to Ram a Hostile Vehicle

There is no way round the aggressor and, though it goes against your nature, you have no alternative but to try and smash a path through. This is fraught with danger and might leave you as well as the assailant incapacitated so really is the action of last resort. Once you've made the decision, here are the steps to follow:

1) Cut your speed as if you're about to stop. Put the car in its lowest gear and deactivate any airbags.

2) Decide where you are going to strike. You want to aim at the lightest part of the hostile vehicle and away from the engine. Your goal is to pivot the vehicle out of your path, so on most vehicles the region between back wheel and back bumper is best.

3) Put your foot on the accelerator and execute your move. Once through, keep driving until you reach safety.

How to Drive Your Way Out of Trouble

It is far preferable to attempt to exit the scenario without engagement. However, it won't be easy and your assailants might well have prepared for such a response. But if you have time, space and faith in your driving capabilities, you may decide to commit to such a course of action. Now you must choose your letter: the J-turn, the Y-turn or the handbrake turn.

1) The J-turn is suited to a cramped area. Having selected a turning point, you will need to slam on the brakes and go into reverse at speed. On hitting the turning point, move the steering wheel through 180° (effectively from 9 o'clock to 3 o'clock) while pressing down on the clutch and brake. The car itself should then spin through 180°, at which point get into

first gear, straighten your steering wheel and drive off hard.

2) Where there is a little more space and time before you hit the ambush, you might opt for the Y-turn. It is a relatively simple manoeuvre in which you brake and reverse into a 90° turn before speeding off (see diagram).

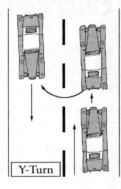

Y-Turn

3) The handbrake turn also requires more time and space. Its big advantage is its effectiveness in throwing off any pursuing cars, but it will briefly put your rear passengers in closer proximity to your ambushers. To execute it, depress the clutch and turn the steering wheel around 10° off your previous course. You then need to spin the wheel through 180° (either from 9 o'clock to 3 o'clock or vice versa). Wait until the vehicle begins its turn before applying the handbrake. You should then spin until you are facing away from your assailants (see diagrams). Release the handbrake but put your foot down on the brake pedal to avoid reversing. Get the car into gear and, as before, make off like there is no tomorrow.

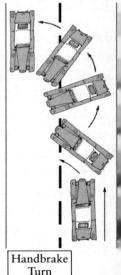

Handbrake
Turn

Emergency First Aid

U nless you are properly qualified, you should always seek timely professional medical attention for an injured party. But it is inevitable that sometimes the situation is so urgent that you cannot wait for the emergency services. If a loved one starts choking at the dinner table or a companion has broken their leg on a mountain ridge, it might fall to you to be a hero. Your aim should be to do what you can to get the patient out of immediate danger and in a situation where experienced medics can do the rest. It is well worth attending a properly accredited first-aid course to prepare for most of the emergency medical situations that you are ever likely to face. In the meantime, familiarize yourself with the techniques described here.

How to Treat Electric Shock

Electricity is all around us in our everyday lives, from the profusion of domestic appliances in our homes to the computers we use at work, the escalators in the shopping centre or the lights in the street. A damaged appliance or some ill-advised tinkering with an electrical item un-isolated from its power source can deliver a most unpleasant shock to the unwary.

If a person comes into contact with an electrical current, it will use their body as a convenient bridge to the earth. You may not be able to feel a very weak electrical current as low as 1 milliampere (mA) but 100 mA can be fatal. A strong enough current can cause serious burns and trigger muscle spasms or cause the heart to stop. Your first instinct on seeing someone suffering from an electric shock will be to rush to their aid. Don't do it. If they still have an electric current flowing through them, it will flow through you as well. There are a few important rules to remember when dealing with the victims of electric shock.

1) Use your eyes. Is the victim still in contact with the source of the electricity? Is he holding a cable or touching an appliance with any part of his body? If so, you must not touch him and you must warn anyone else nearby to stay well back.

2) Isolate the power source. Cut off the power. Switch off at the plug if you can do so safely, or else turn off at the mains.

3) If the person is still in contact with the source after you have switched off the power, or if you are unable to switch it off, you can try to move him away from it but you must ensure that you insulate yourself first. You could stand on a dry rubber mat, a pile of newspapers or a car tyre and use something that will not conduct electricity, like a dry length of timber, a broom handle or a wooden chair, to push to victim clear of the source.

4) When he is clear of the source, extinguish any burning clothing using a jacket, towel or blanket to smother the flames. He may well be unconscious, so check his breathing and pulse. If necessary, perform artificial respiration (see pages 117-19) and chest compressions.

5) Once he is breathing again, check the condition of any burns. Burns should be cleaned with cool or lukewarm water (never cold or iced water) and a sterile burns dressing or a layer of cling film applied. If you do not have these to hand, then leave well alone and call an ambulance.

6) If the victim was thrown clear of the electrical source by muscle spasms or by any kind of blast, check for broken bones. On no account attempt to move the victim. Call for an ambulance.

Any electric-shock victim, whether or not the victim has suffered major burns or lost consciousness, should be taken to hospital for a proper medical check. Internal injuries and other after-effects may not be immediately apparent but must be diagnosed by a professional.

How to Deal with Burns and Scalds

There is a high risk of infection with burns that can be limited by taking sensible precautions, but any burns victim needs to be treated by a medical professional as early as possible. First-aid treatment is straightforward but should be undertaken with great care and using the essential element in any emergency situation – common sense.

1) Stop the burning immediately by removing the casualty from the source of heat. If the victim is on fire, douse him with water or smother the flames with a blanket. Do not put yourself at risk.
2) Reduce the temperature of the burned area of skin using clean, tepid water. Bathe the area with water for up to 30 minutes to limit damage and reduce pain and swelling. Do not use ice, cold water, creams or any greasy agents like butter or moisturizer.
3) Make sure that the victim is kept warm by covering them

with a coat or blanket but do not cover the injured area. This will help to reduce the effects of shock and, in severe conditions, ward off hypothermia.

4) Do not attempt to remove any burnt clothing remnants or fibres from the wound as this may cause more damage. Do remove or cut away any clothing around the burn that might interfere with the wound or that is tight to the skin in the affected area and likely to cause more swelling. Do not burst any blisters that have formed as they provide protection for the wound and do not attempt to remove any loose skin.

5) To prevent infection, the wound should be covered. A sterile dressing should be lightly applied but do not use any kind of bandage that is fluffy or that might introduce more loose fibres to the wound. Cling film can be used to cover burns until the victim can be taken to hospital. Lightly cover the affected area only and do not wrap cling film around a limb as a tight binding can cause swelling. A clean, clear plastic bag can also be useful for burns on hands or feet.

6) Call for an ambulance or get the victim to a hospital.

If the victim has suffered a chemical burn, a dry chemical should be lightly brushed off the skin. Running water should be used to rinse the chemical off the skin. Take care not to come into contact with the substance yourself.

How to Cope with a Broken Limb

Breaking an arm or leg is an intensely painful experience and the only way to ensure a successful recovery is to have the injury attended to by a medical professional. Call the emergency services.

In a survival situation, however, when there is no other help at hand and none likely to be forthcoming, there are a number of things that you should do.

1) Immobilize the patient. Of course, a broken-leg victim is not going to be running around the place, but anyone with an untreated broken arm risks causing more damage and pain if they keep on the move. Have the casualty lie flat on his back to aid circulation and help prevent shock.

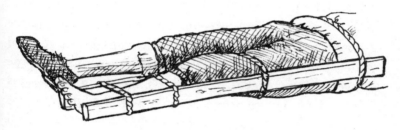

2) Identify the problem. A broken bone in the arm or leg may be obvious, especially if part of the fracture has broken through the skin. Otherwise, you should check for swelling. The skin around the swollen area may also feel warm because of the extra blood. Compare the limb to the unaffected arm or leg. Signs of unnatural angles where you would expect the bones to be straight indicate a fracture. In a break where the ends of the broken bone have not been knocked out of alignment, the swollen area may appear as a kind of 'doughnut' around the limb. Check for function and mobility in the limb. A person with a broken arm may still be able to grip your finger with his hand, but he will not be able to grip as strongly as he can with his unaffected hand. In the case of a broken leg, the

patient will not be able to wiggle the toes as vigorously, if at all. Raising and lowering or rotating the limb will be difficult, painful or impossible with a fractured bone.

3) Immobilize the limb. Once a fracture has been identified, the limb must not be allowed to move around. Movement will cause crepitus (as dreadful as it sounds), where the ends of broken bones grind together. The bone should be set in a splint, which can be made with two straight lengths of stick bound to the limb above and below the broken bone to hold it straight. In the case of a broken leg, if it is too painful to lift the leg, the splints can go on either side. If you don't have any obvious splints (for instance, straight walking sticks, tree branches or ski poles), use a little imagination. Newspaper sheets can be wrapped around a broken arm in several layers, for example, to immobilize the limb very effectively. If nothing can be found to splint the leg, you can bind it to the other leg. Don't be tempted to elevate the limb.

Use some kind of padding – a scarf or sweater wrapped around the limb – to stop the splint from causing discomfort. On the arm the splints should be long enough to run from the elbow to the wrist or, if the break is above the elbow, from the elbow to the shoulder. The arm can then be supported with a sling to avoid further injury. On the leg, it is best to hold the entire limb straight, bound at the thigh, below the knee and at the ankle. You can use rope, strips of torn cloth or belts to bind the splints but do not tie them too tight as this will cut off circulation. You should be able to slip a finger under the binding. Check from time to time that the splinted limb is not turning pale as this may mean the bindings are too tight.

4) Twisted limbs. It may be that the fracture has caused the bone to twist out of position. You will not be able to apply splints effectively if the foot, for example, is facing off at an unnatural angle. In this case you should do your best to make the casualty comfortable until help arrives. If help is not expected, you may be able to use gentle traction to realign the broken bone. You need to pull gently in a straight line with the bone to allow the misaligned end of the bone to move back into position. This will be extremely painful for the casualty, but he may find that after realignment, he is suffering less pain that previously. Remember, this is a procedure only for an extreme emergency. Serious complications can result from trying to manipulate a fracture.

5) If the break caused the skin to be punctured, the wound should be cleaned using clean water and any foreign bodies removed before a sterile dressing is applied. You may need to do this before strapping the splints in place. Again, if help is on the way, make the casualty comfortable and leave the wound to them.

How to Tie a Sling

Tying a sling is an invaluable skill that anyone from childhood up should really learn how to do. Any Cub worth his woggle would certainly be able to tell you how to do it.

What You'll Need

A decently large square cloth (for instance, a bandage or bandana)
A safety pin

How to Do It

1) If your patient has a suspected broken arm, make sure it has been splinted.

2) Fold your cloth in half so it forms a triangle.

3) The top point of the triangle should be at the elbow of the injured arm. The wrist of the injured arm should be positioned a little way along the triangle's long edge.

4) The point nearest this wrist should be brought up over the shoulder of the uninjured arm from the front. The last 'free point' should be brought round to the same shoulder across the back.

5) The two ends should then be tied securely at the shoulder (or pinned). Loose material at the elbow can also be tied off.

6) The forearm of the injured arm should be supported along its length by the sling, which should feel secure.

7) Check for tightness of the sling and loosen if needs be. Keep an eye on the fingers of the injured arm to make sure that circulation, sensation and motion are normal.

How to Give the Kiss of Life

More correctly known as 'artificial respiration', this technique is often used in conjunction with chest compressions in a life-saving procedure known as CPR or Cardio-Pulmonary Resuscitation. This is a technique that can be used when you come across an accident victim who has stopped breathing and whose heart may also have stopped beating. Successful CPR can bring a patient 'back from the dead'. Here is how to check for vital signs and how to perform CPR:

1) Check whether the victim is breathing. With the victim lying on his back, hold your ear close to his mouth. If he is breathing normally, you will be able to hear and feel the flow of air. Look down over his chest and abdomen while you are doing this. You should be able to see the chest rise and fall. If you can feel no flow of air and see no movement, then the victim is not breathing normally.

2) Place one hand behind the neck and the other on the forehead and gently tilt the head back. This helps to open the airways. Leave your hand on the forehead to keep the casualty's head tilted back.

3) Check for obstructions. Open the victim's mouth with your free hand and use two fingers to depress the tongue. Look for any foreign matter or dislodged teeth in the mouth and

4) Introduce oxygen. If the preceding steps have not already caused the victim to start breathing, then you need to get oxygen into his system. The air you breathe out retains a large percentage of the oxygen you breathed in. That is what you will give to the victim. Using the hand that is on the victim's forehead, reach down to his nose with forefinger and thumb to pinch his nostrils shut. There is no point in your breathing air if it shoots out your victim's nose. Take a deep breath, open your mouth wide and seal your lips over the victim's mouth. Breathe out gently (for no more than a couple of seconds) while watching for the victim's chest to rise. Take your mouth away and watch as the chest falls, while holding your ear to the victim's mouth to listen for air to flow out. Then breathe into the victim's mouth again. This technique should be followed until the victim starts to breathe for himself or until the emergency services arrive to take over. If the casualty is a small child, it may be easiest to supply artificial respiration by sealing your lips over the victim's nose and mouth. For an adult victim with a mouth injury, it may be more effective to cover the mouth and provide artificial respiration via the nose.

5) Check for a pulse. When making the initial check on the victim's breathing, you should also check for a heartbeat. Place two fingers on the victim's neck to one side of his windpipe to check the carotid artery. If you can feel no pulse, put your ear to his chest to try to hear or feel a heartbeat. It is important to establish that there is no heartbeat, however faint, before embarking on chest compressions as you can cause damage

by compressing a beating heart.

6) Begin chest compressions. Feel for the breastbone in the middle of the victim's chest, then place the heel of one hand flat on the chest just above the bottom of the breastbone, with your fingers spaced out. Place your other hand on top, letting its fingers sit in the gaps between the ones below. Keeping your elbows rigid, lean forward to bring weight to bear on the victim's chest. The chest should be compressed by about 2 inches (5cm), then you should lean back to release the pressure. You should aim to compress the chest about 80 times per minute. Check the pulse again after every 15 compressions.

7) Combined operations. If the victim has neither a pulse nor the ability to breathe, artificial respiration and chest compressions should be combined. If you have to undertake this alone, you should give the victim two breaths followed by 15 chest compressions. Check heartbeat and breathing after one minute, then resume if there is no improvement. You may have to continue with artificial respiration after the pulse returns.

How to Deal with Choking

While fairly common, choking is extremely unpleasant to experience and can have serious consequences. Your first job is to find out how severe the choking is. Ask the casualty if they are choking. If they respond that they are, you may assume the blockage is mild. You should encourage them to cough up the blockage but should do nothing more. If they cannot speak, or respond only by nodding, it is likely more serious. In these cases, you will also notice breathing problems and any attempts they make at coughing will be silent. In serious instances, they may even lose consciousness. In a case of severe airway obstruction, you should:

1) Give the casualty five blows to the back, with the aim of jarring the obstruction free. For maximum effect, the casualty should be bent over with their head lowered forward. You should stand behind and to one side, using the heel of your hand to strike between the shoulder blades. Check after every strike to see if it's done the trick..

2) If this method doesn't work, you will need to execute the abdominal thrust. Standing or kneeling behind the casualty, place one fist (with the thumb end against the casualty) around the upper abdomen in the region above the navel and below the point of the breastbone. With your other hand, grasp the fist and in a sharp stroke, pull back and up (at an angle of 45^0 to the horizontal). Make five thrusts, and then try five further blows on the back, repeating until the obstruction moves or the patient loses consciousness.

3) If the casualty has lost consciousness, you need to lower them gently to the floor, call an ambulance, and start emergency CPR (See page 117) until the victim's breathing is under control.

How to Deal with Splinters and Blisters

Splinters and blisters might be reasonably low-level on the 'serious injuries' scale but they can easily bring a tear to the eye of even the toughest man and bring an end to the fun on a weekend jaunt. More often than not, you won't need to resort to specialist medical attention, but you do need to know how to deal with their particular challenges correctly.

How to Get a Splinter Out

What You'll Need

Tweezers
A plaster or bandage
A needle
Alcohol or a match

How to Do It

1) First and foremost, wash your hands with soap and water and then wash around the problem area.
2) In the best case scenario, one end of the splinter will be protruding from your skin and you'll be able to grip it with the tweezers and slowly remove it from the flesh.

3) Once the splinter is out, rewash the area and apply a plaster or bandage.

4) If a splinter is entirely embedded, things are more complicated and likely to be more painful. Be strong, men!

5) You will need to create a hole in the skin through which the splinter can pass out. Do this using a combination of a sterilized needle and tweezers.

6) To sterilize the needle, wash it in alcohol or hold it in the flame of a match for a few seconds. Let it cool down and clean away any carbon deposit.

7) You may feel slightly woozy in the process of removing a splinter. If you still don't have any success, a trip to the doctor is on the cards.

8) Be warned, if a wooden splinter gets moist for too long, it can swell up and cause additional irritation. Any splinter left unattended may also become infected. Look out for: swelling; red, inflamed skin; pus; a feeling of heat around the splinter. Read the signs and get yourself off to the local surgery. And, of course, a splinter in the eye requires immediate emergency treatment from a qualified medic.

How to Treat Blisters

What You'll Need

Scissors
Foot powder
A blister plaster
Lubricant (such as petroleum jelly)

How to Do It

1) The best way to deal with a blister is not to get one in the first place. Wear comfortable, well-fitting shoes suited to the terrain you'll be facing. Choose a breathable sock (seamless) to go directly on the foot, and a durable woollen sock to go on top of it.

2) If the worst happens despite your precautions, treat a blister early. The longer you leave it, the worse it will get. If you can feel a blister coming but it has not yet appeared, put a suitable lubricant on your feet and top with a liberal sprinkling of foot powder. This should reduce friction on the delicate area.

3) Cut out a blister pad that is slightly bigger than the blister itself. Then cut out a hole in the middle of the pad the same size as the blister.

4) Put the pad on, with the hole over the blister. This lets the area breathe while the pad will stop your footwear from rubbing it.

5) If you're out hiking, change your socks every few hours. Sweaty socks will moisten the blister, when to heal it needs to dry out.

6) Most blisters can be kept under control, but if not treated properly and allowed to heal they can become infected and cause serious problems. You will then require professional attention. A bit of common sense and you should never get to that stage.

How to Deal with a Panic Attack

Caused by extreme anxiety, panic attacks rarely cause serious harm but are extremely unpleasant for those suffering.

How to Recognize a Panic Attack

1) Does the person seem excessively apprehensive or anxious?
2) Are they hyperventilating?
3) Are they sweating and shivering/trembling?
4) Is their pulse rate fast?
5) Is their mouth dry?
6) Are they having palpitations?

What to Do

1) Move the casualty into a quiet and calm space, away from lots of people.
2) Attempt to calm them down by explaining that they are suffering a panic attack and that they will be all right.
3) Try to establish a medical history. Has this happened to them before? Is there an obvious trigger that has brought on the present attack?
4) Urge them to bring their breathing under control, taking slow, controlled breaths. Breathing into a paper bag or into cupped hands are both effective ways of regulating a person's breathing pattern.
5) Remain with the casualty until the attack is over.
6) Encourage them to seek a medical check-up.

How to Cope with Suspected Poisoning

The most common method of poisoning is through swallowing, either of an intrinsically toxic substance or a substance, such as alcohol, that is only poisonous in abnormal doses. Poisons ingested in such a manner can be subdivided into two types: corrosive and systemic.

Corrosive poisons will burn the body's tissues and are likely to do their damage in the mouth and throat, with the potential to cause serious problems in the airways. If you or someone you encounter has swallowed a corrosive poison, your first aim is to wash out the mouth to limit the immediate damage, get to a hospital as soon as possible and continue drinking water en route. Though you might be tempted to try and get rid of the poison by vomiting, this will only cause further burning and should not be attempted. While you should do whatever you can for the casualty, don't put yourself in any danger in the process.

Systemic poisons are those which attack, as the name suggests, the body's systems. These may include alcohol or medications taken in excess, either accidentally or on purpose. This is your classic overdose case and there will normally be a time delay, unlike corrosive poisons, between ingestion and symptoms. On discovering an overdose victim, you must first establish what level of consciousness they have, whether they are still breathing and if their airways are obstructed. Put the casualty into the recovery position if needed, search out emergency medical assistance and make note of all relevant information you can, whether garnered directly from the casualty, or by observing symptoms or physical evidence from the scene (for instance, what substance(s) they have consumed).

Dealing with Animals

Man, the great naked ape, has not always played fair with animals, from hunting and cooking them, to putting them in cages to be stared at and prodded, to dressing them up in ridiculous clothes for our amusement or to compensate for a personality deficiency. The animal world, in comparison, has been very good to us. By and large, we humans are the ones to take on the role of predator while other species are quite happy to give us a wide berth unless we have really done something to gee them up. However, there are rare occasions when we find ourselves in a surprise one-on-one situation with a creature and the odds can look frighteningly stacked in their favour. Few of us can hope to out-muscle a bull, tickle an alligator into submission or take a snake bite without consequences. What we can perhaps hope for is that we have the upper hand intellectually. Read on so that, should the situation arise, you are at least armed with foreknowledge.

How to Escape from a Bear

Rupert, Paddington, Winnie the Pooh – you could doubtless paste any of them should you get into an argument over a pot of honey or a marmalade sandwich. However, get a bear on his own in the wild and you should feel considerably less confident. As is so often the way, your main aim should be to avoid a confrontation. Bears are rather shy fellows by nature and they won't generally come looking for trouble. If you find yourself in bear country, make a bit of noise to announce your presence. You might do this by chatting away volubly or by singing songs (perhaps a verse of two of 'The Teddy Bears' Picnic') and you can even buy 'bear bells'. If they know you're there, they will try to steer clear of you.

The quickest way to attract a bear's unwanted attention is to offer something he wants – by and large, this will be food. Make sure any supplies are stored away and always keep a tidy camp, with any waste properly disposed of. Give the bear no reason to come and explore your immediate territory. If you come across bear tracks, seek an alternative route, having put any dogs with you on a lead. Definitely don't creep up on a bear and don't get between a female and her cubs. Like all good mums, her babies are her priority and she'll go after anything she thinks might be a threat to them.

If you see a bear in the distance, get out of the area as quickly as possible. Even if it ruins the plans you had or involves a long detour, exit the scene. When you are out of harm's way, make lots of noise as you go on your way to lengthen the odds of a further chance meeting.

If you are somewhat nearer and a bear has clocked you, reverse away slowly, speaking in a low and calm tone (the words you use are entirely irrelevant, anything will do, but make sure you don't whistle) and avoiding direct eye contact (although keep an eye on what it is up to). You want to show that you mean no harm, but that you can handle yourself too, so do not cower.

If the bear decides to come towards you, make yourself as big as you can while continuing your attempt to back away slowly and speak calmly. However, if the bear continues its approach, stop still and show you will not be cowed. Continue speaking in the same tone but raise the volume. Wave your arms around so that you seem bigger. Don't be aggressive but make yourself appear strong and determined. And if the furry one charges you, stay where you are. The chances are it is just trying it on and will back off before he reaches you.

You must make a split-second decision as to the bear's motivation for approaching you. Is it predatory (i.e. it sees you as a hearty snack) or defensive (you've strayed across each other's paths or it fears for its young)?

Playing dead in a non-predatory attack is an option only with grizzlies or polar bears and only after the bear has actually contacted you or made a concerted effort to do so. You should lie flat on the ground, protecting your most vital parts as much as possible and shielding your neck with your arms. Keep still, even if the bear makes a check of you. Wait till the bear has left the scene and been gone for at least a few minutes before beating your own retreat.

If the attack is predatory (and in any type of encounter with a black bear), you will need to fight back. You need to frighten it off so use any weapons that come to hand – rocks, camping equipment, sticks, your own body. With a bit of luck the bear will be so shocked to find itself in a scuffle that it will back off and leave you to escape.

Your alternative is the old 'up a tree' routine. You won't outrun a bear, so you'll need to be close to a suitable tree in the first place. The technique won't work with a black bear, but if you can get significantly higher than 20 feet you stand a chance of outclimbing a grizzly. Otherwise, you might choose to run, but if you do so, run in a zigzag to force your pursuer to change direction (not a particular strength for most bears). Remember, though, that this will tire you out as well as the bear, and in a straight sprint you don't stand a chance. Finally, if you know you are going into bear territory, get expert advice on the efficacy of specific bear sprays, which can prove a useful weapon.

How to Fight Off an Alligator

Just as with bears, an alligator is most likely to strike at dusk and in the early part of the evening. Thankfully, attacks are equally rare. Perhaps more than with any other creature, you should really aim to avoid an encounter in the first place. Once battle commences, you have some hope of survival, but you might want to get yourself ready to familiarize yourself with the 'gator's belly.

You should have a pretty good idea of when you're near alligator territory. Their natural habitat is tropical, swampy climes, so take comfort from the fact that you're unlikely to bump into one on your trip to the local shops. If you are in 'gator territory, stay away from the areas they inhabit, particularly during the perilous twilight hours and during the summer months (when they are most active). If you are fishing near alligator territory, don't think about cleaning fish at the waterside as you may draw unwanted attention to yourself.

In some parts of the world, such as in Florida, there are reasonably regular reports of attacks on golfers playing on courses close to danger areas. If you find yourself teeing off in the Everglades, don't be tempted to wade into any potentially inhabited waters in search of your mis-hit drive. Similarly, if you have any domestic pets with you, keep them away from the water's edge. Give the alligators no extra incentive to come and investigate. Never feed them, don't actively get in their way and if you want to observe them, do so from a safe distance. Be sure to abide by any signs concerning swimming restrictions. Alligators are good at keeping a low profile in the water and are very difficult to spot. If you are in an area where they are known to hide out, be extra vigilant.

Alligators don't generally dine on humans but that is not to say that you won't appeal to a maverick creature. If, despite all your best efforts, you find you've tickled the taste buds of one, obey the following rules:

1) Make lots of noise and move around a lot. In a best case scenario, the alligator will be put off altogether and slope off to find something less problematic to munch on.

2) If you are far enough away from your opponent on land, you have a reasonable chance of outrunning it. 'Gators like to rely on the element of surprise in an attack and are not so keen on a pursuit. However, they can be nippy on land and you definitely won't be able to outswim one. Adopt the 'running away' defence only if you have distance on your side.

3) If you are attacked, fight back. No point just giving in. The chances are that your attacker wants to drag you underwater and put you in a death roll. You will stand little chance then but to have any hope, go with the roll. Really, you must do everything in your power to avoid entering the water with the animal. Fortunately, the alligator does have some vulnerabilities. Go for its eyes, hitting or poking with your fingers or with any weapon you have to hand. The nostrils and ears are good secondary targets if you can cut them or hit them hard enough. There is also a flap of tissue behind the alligator's tongue, which prevents it from drowning when submerged. If your arm or leg has found its way into the creature's throat, aim for this flap. If you get a good contact, the beast will instinctively release you.

4) Once you have escaped the set-to, get medical attention. You will need it.

It is worth remembering that in an attack situation, what is good for a 'gator works for a crocodile too.

How to Treat a Snake-bite

It may be scant reassurance to learn that less than half of all snake-bites are poisonous. If you are not sure whether a bite is venomous, act as if it were. If at all possible, kill the snake that bit or get a description of it to assist the medical services later. Then follow these rules:

1) Seek qualified help immediately.
2) Do your utmost to keep the casualty calm. Get them to lie

down quietly until help arrives. Keep them warm and make sure the area of the bite is below the level of the heart.

3) If help is unlikely to arrive within half an hour, do you have a snake-bite kit with you? Clean away any excess venom. You might use a venom pump, although debate rages as to their use. As venom works via the circulation of the blood, you can attempt to suck out the poison without risk as long as you have no open wounds in your mouth. Again, though, there is some doubt as to the benefits of this approach. You definitely should not attempt to 'cut out' the wounded area, as you'll succeed only in exposing more blood to the poison.

4) If the bite is on the arm or leg, tie a bandage reasonably snugly a few inches above the bite (but not over it). The wounded area must be immobilized.

5) If you are not sure help can get to you, you must try to get to it. Snake-bites can be fatal and the casualty may need a specific anti-venom.

How to Defend Yourself in a Shark Attack

The movie *Jaws* has much to answer for – by no means is every shark a finned assassin. It is said that you have more chance of being killed by a hippo than a shark but, as ever, we do not let the truth get in the way of a good story.

Though it happens rarely, sharks can nonetheless be a threat on occasion, mostly at twilight or night-time. If you are swimming in a group when you become aware of some unwanted interest, you should form yourselves into a tight ring facing outwards. Sharks don't like a crowd. Nor are they fond of loud noises and strong, rhythmical movements, so try slapping your cupped hands into the water if one is getting close.

Should you lack the safety of numbers, it is imperative you stay calm. Not to put too fine a point on it, soiling yourself will only attract the attentions of a shark. Swim rhythmically and don't be tempted to play dead – you will just make yourself more vulnerable. If you can, rid yourself of anything shiny on your personage, such as jewellery, as the shark may take this to be a fish of some type. If you think the shark is not an imminent threat, try to make for dry land as quickly as possible. Otherwise, check if there is anywhere to hide, such as in reeds. Your next best option is to head to the ocean floor, if you have suitable breathing equipment.

If a set-to ensues, hit it with any object that comes to hand. For instance, if you are out diving you might have a camera. Using an object to hit with keeps your hands that little bit further from danger. But if you don't have anything, use your feet to kick the animal or punch it with a stiff arm and the heel of your hand.

Aim for the nose, eyes and gills – your opponent's most vulnerable areas. When you strike, do it like you mean it. As long as you're not contending with a giant, you stand a good chance of winning a dust-up.

How to Break Up a Dog Fight

Treated well, a dog will be a man's best friend, it is true. But today, as throughout history, people lacking a bit of bite themselves have bred dogs to have it for them. Aggressive dogs are a major problem in many societies, kept to intimidate or, in some instances, to take part in illegal dog fights. More rarely, an otherwise quiet and peaceful hound might suddenly turn. The cumulative result is that dog fights are not an uncommon sight on our streets and in our parks. Breaking up a clash is not without significant risk but you might judge it to be essential to intervene. Here's how to do it:

1) Do not try to get in the middle of the fight. Even if they are two beloved pets, in the moment of the set-to they are animals fighting for their lives. You won't instantly be recognized as their darling master. You are more likely to get bitten.

2) A bucket of cold water or a brisk hose-down is likely to shatter even the strongest fighting instinct.

3) If that is not an option, attempt to separate the animals using a large bit of board, a stout stick or a net. You might then need to use it to keep the put-out dog away from you.

4) Otherwise, try making a very loud noise (several blasts are better than one long din) to distract them, such as with an airhorn.

5) Once the fighting breaks up, try to get the dogs away from

each other, though maintaining your own safety at all times. Is it possible to get one of the dogs into a separate room or into a car?

6) Is there someone to hand who can help you? As a last resort, each of you picks a dog, approaches them from behind and seizes the back legs. With the hounds in a wheelbarrow position, the animals are pulled apart and led away from each other. You will need to be vigilant that the dogs can't immediately resume their scrap as soon as you let go and also that you aren't at risk of being bitten yourself. Sweeping the 'wheelbarrow' in a circular motion as you back away may give you some extra protection.

How to Deal with an Aggressive Dog

It might be that you find yourself the victim of a dog attack. There are a couple of things you can do to avoid a confrontation, so keep them in mind.

1) Never goad a dog. You may get more than you bargained for. Avoid smiling, too. A kindly gesture among humans it may be, but to a dog you are baring your teeth.
2) Some dogs are obviously ferocious but all dogs have that capability. Pick up on any signs that a canine is getting fractious.

In the case of an actual attack:

1) Stay calm and show it. Panicking may either egg the dog on or be misread as aggression from you. Don't try to run

    – the pursuit will seem like great sport and you won't win the race.

2)   Try some basic commands: 'Down!' or 'Go home!' are both worth a try. Hopefully the dog will remember his place in the natural order.

3)   Stand sideways on to the dog and avoid eye contact to seem less threatening. Cross your arms and keep your hands tucked away, or keep your arms to your side, with fingers out of harm's way.

4)   Stand your ground. Having adopted a non-aggressive stance the dog will hopefully soon get distracted by a new sound or strange smell. Even if the dog comes over to sniff you out, stay still. Sniffing is fine; it's only the biting side of things that we want to avoid.

5)   If the dog is intent on attacking you, get into a protective foetal position on the ground. Protect the vulnerable neck and face areas with your hands and arms and curl up like a ball. Don't thrash about and keep quiet. The dog will eventually lose interest. Once the danger has passed, get up and get some medical help. On no account leave a dog bite unattended.

If you discover someone else being attacked, don't be tempted to drag the victim away. This might result in worsening bite wounds. If you have a stick or something similar close by, hit the dog across the back of the neck or across its nose. Don't go for the rest of the head as you'll only make him angrier. Alternatively, try to force an object into the dog's mouth. This might even be your own arm, if you have managed to wrap it in some protection (a coat or thick jumper, for instance). If you do choose this course of action, be decisive and force it hard into the dog's jaw.

How to Deal with an Angry Bull

You've had a thoroughly enjoyable hike through the countryside, perhaps stopping off at an inn or two for a reviving pint along the way. You're all set to make your way back to base when the calm of your day is shattered. You have stepped into a field only to be confronted by an angry bull. But play things the right way and you should be able to make your escape, armed with a story to share for many moons to come.

What to Do

1) If you see the bull early, exit swiftly from the field. As with any other animal, best not to get to the point of confrontation.

2) If you have no option but to go through the field, consider the situation. Are there cows around? If so, the bull might not be so aggressive. Has he seen you? Is he exhibiting aggressive behaviour (such as putting his head down, arching his neck and hoofing the ground)? If he is, do all you can to find an alternative route.

3) If you opt to go through the field, keep an eye on the bull but try to keep out of his sight line. He will respond to movement.

4) If your attempts at discretion fail and the bull charges you, run away if you have time. Make for the nearest feasible exit and launch yourself out of harm's way. If you have a dog with you, let it off the lead. The dog will, God willing, manage to

outrun the bull and will distract attention away from you.

5)   If you don't have time to outrun the bull (they are very quick over short distances), you will need to distract him. Though not a recommended way to start your career as a matador, now is your chance to shine. Take off a piece of clothing (and don't dally over this). Hold it to your side and shake it, bull-fighter style. The bull will make for the area of this movement. As late as your nerves will allow, fling the garment away from you and the bull should continue after it, leaving you with precious seconds to manufacture an escape.

How to Fend Off a Leech Attack

It's a horror-film scenario. You're wading through the wilds when you feel something unpleasant. You look down at your body and adhering to it is an army of blood-sucking killer slugs. Leeches!

In truth, they aren't going to consume your whole being there and then, but they do carry a host of nasty bacteria and viruses, they are feasting on your blood and they aren't going to give up without a fight. Your first instinct is, no doubt, to rip the blighters off you – but that is entirely the wrong thing to do. While you might tear away the big part of them, you'll end up with bits of their jaws left in your flesh, ripe for infection. The other common response is to throw salt on them or burn them off with a flame. While either ploy should remove them, they'll vomit up the blood they have just sucked back into your bloodstream, but now 'enriched' with a multitude of nasty bacteria. Instead, follow these rules:

1) Leeches inhabit damp environments, from marshes and swaps to rainforests, and if you take yourself on to their manor, they will hear you and then smell you. Then they will come for you. If you're in an environment where they are known, dress sensibly and coat yourself in insect repellent to put them off.

2) If you are in an area where they are likely to be, keep checking your skin to make sure they haven't already taken a bite into you.

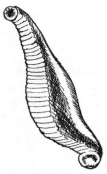

3) If you catch one on you, you want to scrape it off. Do this by sliding a fingernail sideways under its 'oral sucker', located at its thin end, and scrape slowly.

4) Having lifted away the thin end, slide your finger promptly under its fat end to remove it entirely. The leech won't give up easily but you should be able to win through.

5) At an opportune moment, check the rest of your body. Where one begins, others are likely to follow.

6) Clean any wounds and ensure that they don't become infected.

How to Treat a Jellyfish Sting

Jellyfish can be silent predators, unleashing their venomous tentacles against you as you innocently lark around in the sea. Often you will get away with nothing more than a nasty sting, but should you find yourself in a prolonged encounter with a box jellyfish or a Portuguese man-of-war, your life might be under threat. If you are the victim of an attack, seek out expert help at the earliest opportunity.

Your first objective is to remove the tentacles from the casualty's skin. Do this by applying hot water if you can, or salt water otherwise. Cooler fresh water might increase the pain. Take off any remaining tentacles with a gloved hand, a stick, tweezers or similar. Make sure they don't get on you or your clothes.

Check the casualty is not suffering an anaphylaxis (an allergic reaction). Symptoms include itching, hives, shortness of breath/wheezing, a tight throat, flushed skin and general weakness. The wound should then be submerged in water as hot as the casualty can cope with. Applying a liberal dose of vinegar will also reduce pain. However, be warned. While vinegar helps in most cases, it will make the sting of certain types of man-of-war worse. If you have been attacked by that particular species, seek immediate medical attention. If it's available, put some ice on the wound to cool it down and reduce the pain.

Coping with the Unexpected

How to Escape from a Burning Building

Most assuredly, you don't want to find yourself amid a blazing inferno before you start to think about how you might extricate yourself and any companions. As ever, you will be at a considerable advantage if you have made some preparation ahead of any emergency. In your own home, make sure you fit fire and smoke alarms. Don't leave them to their own accord and assume that they'll come to your rescue when you need them – test them every week to make sure they are in working order. In whatever building you find yourself, make sure you are aware of exit routes which will offer you an unobstructed path to safety. Think about how you will help small children to escape – you will, of course, need to lower them out of any high windows before you yourself exit a building. Older children should be made aware that their priority in the event of a fire is to make an escape, rather than take refuge under a bed or in a cupboard. Should the worst happen and a blaze take grip, here's what to do:

1) Naturally enough, your first priority must be to get out of the burning building. If you can do this easily, do not delay. It is not worth contemplating even for a second trying to save any property.

2) It is estimated that between 50–80 per cent of deaths in fires are the result of smoke inhalation rather than burns. As smoke rises, you should get as low to the ground as possible and begin to crawl to the exit, covering your nose and mouth with your hand or, better still, a damp cloth.

3) If you come to a door, touch it with the back of your hand. If it is cool, make your way through and immediately close it again. If it feels hot, seek out an alternative route. If none is available, open the door so it is just ajar but be ready to shut it again if the fire is blocking your path through.

4) If you cannot find any viable escape route, close as many doors as you can between you and the fire to provide you with a barrier against the heat and smoke while you await rescue.

5) If you are able to get away from the building, you should make for a pre-arranged meeting point.

6) No matter how strong the temptation, do not use a lift in a burning multi-storey construction. And under no circumstance should you ever re-enter a blazing building.

How to Talk Your Way Out of a Fight

Man is but a few steps on from the Neanderthal and every now and again we revert to the caveman. A misplaced word, a misinterpreted glance, a spilt pint, a flash of the green-eyed monster . . . it is all too easy to forget that we are civilized gentlemen (especially when we are in cups), instead turning to a sharp right-hook as a means of communicating our annoyance. But the language of the fists is never one that the modern man should turn to. If you find yourself with your back to the wall as tempers flare, try talking your way to safety instead.

How to Do It

1) Never pick a fight. However bad a day you've had, or how much alcohol you've consumed, or how wronged you feel, do not be the aggressor. If you have really been wronged, seek justice by recourse to official channels (if the situation warrants it) or lay out your grievances calmly and succinctly. You never know, if you are in the right, your opponent may even admit as such and seek to right the wrong. As soon as you initiate violence, you have lost the moral high ground.

2) If someone is looking for a fight, perhaps to impress his mates or a female companion, try to ignore him as much as possible. If someone is jostling you in a bar in order to get a reaction out of you, do not satisfy them by rising to the bait. There are limits, of course, to anybody's patience but moving yourself away from a random idiot will serve you well in the long run.

3) Can a situation be redeemed by your actions? If you have

wronged him, can you make amends? For instance, if you were inadvertently chatting up another fellow's girl, offer an apology, explain the mix-up and execute a tactical retreat. If you have clumsily knocked his pint of Best from the bar, consider buying him a replacement.

4) If your adversary is unlikely to be reasoned out of his aggression, try not to escalate matters. Don't use inflammatory language. If you want to avoid a punch-up, explain: 'Look, I don't want any trouble.' Do not qualify the comment by calling him 'an ugly, fat, four-eyed gonk' or similar. Equally, steer away from incendiary subjects. For instance, if you've spilt his pint, don't try to divert him by getting him on to the subject of football if you're a Town fan and he's got a United tattoo on his forehead. You're aiming to lessen the tension, not heighten it.

5) Don't point or make aggressive gestures at your adversary. If you make him feel under physical threat, fisticuffs is likely to occur all the quicker.

6) Keep calm, even if those around you are losing their heads. This, after all, is what makes you a man, according to Rudyard Kipling. Once a 'moment' has ended, do not simmer it within you. Move on with your life. It is far too short not to.

7) If someone openly challenges you to a fight, walk away from it. Whatever they may have to say on the subject, you are being the bigger man and not stooping to their level. The chances are your adversary is quite pleased himself that he will not have to fight.

8) Offer the hand of friendship. If someone is looking for trouble and you offer them peace, they will look rather churlish not

to accept it. A handshake (and even an inoffensive joke, if the situation allows) is a far happier outcome.

9) If your adversary is intent on violence, try to get to a place of safety and seek help from a suitable source (a nightclub bouncer, a policeman, the pack of the local rugby team) to bring the violence to an end, with damage to property and life on all sides kept to an absolute minimum.

How to Fend Off a Frontal Attack

Sadly, life is not fair and, however much you try to avoid it, trouble can come looking for you. For instance, you are walking down an alleyway late at night and somebody has it in mind that they are going to attack you. You are sure no amount of talking will persuade them otherwise. If they are after your wallet, your best bet is to hand it over and make your escape uninjured. Bank cards can be replaced, but your life cannot. However, you may judge that your attacker is intent on causing you serious harm regardless. In such an instance, it pays to have a little knowledge of some self-defence. Your goal is to launch a counter-attack that allows you to escape serious harm and make for a safe place. To achieve this, you will need to be decisive and positive in your actions, even if you are feeling anything but.

The inherent advantage of an attack from the front, as opposed to one from behind, is that you are likely to see it coming, giving you a precious moment or two to decide on a course of action. Here is one well-proven set of tactics:

1) As your attacker gets close to you, he may well make a grab for your wrist and attempt to invade your personal space with his free hand. This threatening behaviour is designed to surprise you and force you into compliance.

2) You should immediately alter this balance of power by breaking free of his grasp and slapping his hands away to the side.

3) Assuming the assailant doesn't then give up the enterprise for a bad lot, you want to put him on the back foot. If you can get hold of his fingers, bend them back. Spitting in his eyes should also take him off guard. Shouting loudly serves several purposes. Not only will it hopefully attract assistance, but the attacker will also be disorientated by the noise and it may add extra gusto to your counter-attack.

4) As any man can tell you, a knee to the groin is a most disabling action.

5) As he lurches forward in pain, aim a right elbow to the nose, throat or temple.

6) By now you will have wrestled some of the initiative from the attacker. Take a swift step backwards and, if he is bent towards you, raise a knee into a delicate area such as his face or throat.

7) With your strongest foot, stamp hard against the assailant's knee.

8) With a bit of luck, he will now be doubled up in pain. Move towards him and drop your elbow down on the back of his head or his neck.

9) Push the attacker away, ideally on to the ground, and if you have created a safe path through, make your escape.

One last word: having driven off or incapacitated your assailant, leave it at that. Any attempt to exact revenge by inflicting more damage on him might well result in a criminal charge of assault. Call the police instead.

How to Fend Off an Attack from the Rear

The rules of engagement in an attack from behind, as might occur in an alleyway or while you are at a cashpoint, are considerably different. By its very nature, the attack is likely to come as a complete shock to you. It is imperative that you burst into defensive action immediately:

1) Elbow your attacker with as much force as you can muster into his ribs.

2) With your attacker in pain and off balance, attempt to get hold of some of his fingers (ring and little finger are most vulnerable). Wrench them back as far as possible and break them if you can. Your attacker will be at a considerable disadvantage without the use of one of his hands.

3) While keeping hold of the hand, you should be able to pivot to face him. Try to expose his centre line, keeping up the

work on the fingers all the while.

4) With your spare hand, consider whether you can get hold of his hair while maintaining pressure on the fingers with the other hand. If you can, grab his hair and pull the head backwards, bringing him closer to the ground.

5) As his knees bend, stamp on the back of his nearest knee, driving him into the ground.

6) While keeping a firm grip on him, shift your momentum forwards and shove him hard into the ground. Make your escape.

Of course, in the heat of battle, things might not go so straightforwardly to plan. Once you have engaged the attacker, be prepared to fight hard and to be flexible in your tactics. Remember, the aim is to get away unharmed by whatever means you can.

Dressing the Part

If a chap is going to deal with whatever situation fate might throw at him, it is important that he looks and feels up to the job. Of course, your attire will depend on your environment; there is no point thinking you can dress the same way for a walk in the countryside as you do for a trek through the Amazon or a climb up Mount Everest. The information contained within this chapter is not geared to coping in extreme conditions. Rather, it is a guide to how to dress practically and look like a gent while enjoying a gentle day in the great outdoors.

How to Choose Your Wardrobe

In better days not so long ago, a gentleman contemplating some healthy fresh air and a leisurely ramble or brisk stroll in the autumn countryside, perhaps even a bicycle excursion to a country inn for lunch, would have known precisely what to wear. He would have exchanged his lounge suit or business attire, polished Oxfords and bowler hat for a set of tweeds, a stout pair of brogues or sturdy walking boots and a tweed cap. All of his clothes, of course, would have been made from natural material – wool, cotton or leather – and those specifically designed for rugged outdoor wear would have served their purpose very well.

The fact is, they still would today. While modern specialist fabrics can justifiably claim to be lighter weight, more waterproof and often less expensive than good quality traditional garments, that doesn't always make them better. Indeed, the very properties that modern fabrics boast of as 'technical' innovations are based on exactly what natural materials have always done.

Let us begin with undergarments. A cotton undershirt or vest, cotton underpants and cotton or woollen socks will always see you right. Cotton, like modern breathable fabrics, is comfortable against the skin. It is soft and not inclined to chafe or rub at seams, will soak up sweat and, because of the air in the natural fibres and trapped in the weave of the fabric, will dry out quickly. As far as socks go, a good pair of woollen socks are even better at moisture control than cotton.

Next on goes a shirt in a heavier cotton than the underwear, but blessed with much the same properties. The air held in the fabric means that it will be warm in cool weather and cooler in warm weather. For trousers, why not opt for the bottom portion of a handsome (and warming) tweed suit? Alternatively, knee-breeches or plus fours have certain advantages. Full-length trousers might be warmer and feel more civilized once you have made it to your country inn, but a walk across muddy fields can leave them wet and marked. Plus fours ending just below the knee are worn with long socks, blocking moisture from seeping up the leg and protecting from unsightly oil stains if you've been on the bike.

It goes without saying that a chap must not consider going out for any length of time without a tie. A knitted woollen number is ideal for a country walk, keeping your neck warm by sealing in heat that would otherwise escape through the gap between your shirt collar and neck. It is also extremely useful in an emergency as a makeshift sling or for binding a splint on a broken limb. A waistcoat is optional, but a carefully selected one will have neat pockets, ideal for carrying useful small items such as safety pins, matches or loose change.

A robust tweed jacket completes the look, the wool weave able to repel water from a light shower and, in prolonged exposure to damp conditions, able to absorb up to 30 per cent of its weight in moisture without really feeling wet. Even when thoroughly wet, it will still keep you warm. In addition, it can shrug off attacks from the thorns of brambles.

As for footwear, you cannot do better than a pair of stout brogues (or walking boots if intending to venture cross-country, into the woods or out on to a hillside). A good leather works like cotton and wool to absorb moisture created by the body, allowing socks to do their job and keep your feet as dry as possible. If the weather looks showery or blustery, shrug on an overcoat – perhaps a traditional 'Ulster' – and complete the look with a tweed cap.

You may be more used to your breathable fabrics, denim and fleeces, day-glo Lycra, body warmers and trainers, but the gent of yore really knew how to set off for a day out with style, comfort and safety in mind.

How to Look After Your Shoes

A good pair of leather shoes for everyday wear should last many years if cared for properly, making the initial investment in what might at first appear to be prohibitively expensive footwear well worthwhile over the life of the shoes. Leather, being animal hide, is a material that 'breathes'. By absorbing moisture from the feet, it helps to keep your feet dry and avoid foot problems caused by bacteria that thrive in a warm, moist environment.

When choosing a shoe, ensure it fits properly. When trying them on, wear the type of sock you would expect to wear with them. If you intend to walk in them with thick woollen socks, there is no point test-driving them in thin cotton ones. With too much room in the shoe, your foot will move around, rubbing at the heel and causing blisters. Your feet expand with walking around during the course of the day, so it is best to try on shoes later in the afternoon. Although leather shoes can stretch a little over time, you should make sure that they are not too tight and that your big toe has up to a thumb's width of space in front of it. You should be able to flex your toes freely inside the shoe.

To keep your new leather shoes looking pristine, keep shoe trees in them while they are not being worn. Cedar wood is best as it absorbs perspiration or moisture that has accumulated in the leather, helping the shoe to dry out naturally. This will also help to maintain the shape and avoid creases in the leather which can lead to cracking. Having wiped off any dirt or mud with a soft damp cloth, you should refrain from polishing your shoes until they have relaxed on the tree, cooled down and dried out. Shoes should always be left to dry naturally, even if they have been exposed to a torrential downpour of rain. Drying shoes in front of a fire or other heat source will lead to the leather developing cracks.

When they are ready to be cleaned, remove any dirt or dust on the shoes with a soft cloth or brush. Salt stains – unsightly white marks on the leather – can be removed using a mixture consisting of a tablespoon of white vinegar diluted in a cup of hot water. This should be gently rubbed over the white marks with a soft cloth and the shoe then allowed to dry.

Shoes that will be exposed to wet weather conditions can be treated with dubbin. This mixture of wax, oil and tallow has been used for hundreds of years to waterproof leather. Dubbin should be rubbed into the leather, with special attention paid to seams and welts, and allowed to dry. However, while an excellent waterproofing agent, it does not impart a shine in the same way that a traditional shoe polish will. Under most normal circumstances, a good polish, which penetrates the leather, moisturizing it to keep it supple, will provide sufficient waterproof protection on its own, without dubbin.

There are many home-made supposed alternatives to traditional shoe polish, such as using banana skins to clean your shoes. None really work as well. Even proprietary 'shoe-wipes' or liquid polish applicators only really work as emergency alternatives as they do not penetrate the leather as thoroughly as polish. Apply the polish straight from the tin using a soft cloth or shoe brush, working it into the leather using a circular motion. A little polish will go a long way. Leave it for a few seconds to settle, then buff the shoe with a soft shoe brush until you have an even shine. Finish off with a final buff using a soft, clean cloth. Do not be tempted to try to achieve the 'spit-and-polish' parade-ground mirror shine you see on guardsmen's dress boots. Leather that is treated in this way becomes overloaded with wax and any old soldier will tell you that, when forced to wear 'best boots' on long marches or in combat, they very quickly cracked and started to fall apart.

How to Stitch a Hem

There has been an unfortunate fashion in recent years of wearing trousers so long that the bottoms of the trouser legs trail along the ground. Before long, this will result in the material fraying, tearing and looking extremely unsightly. With wider trouser legs there is a further danger of the trailing edges catching in escalators, or of you simply standing on one and tripping yourself up. The answer is to effect a quick and simple DIY alteration by shortening the leg length. This operation need take no longer than about half an hour.

What You'll Need

One pair of over-long trousers
One iron and ironing board
One measuring tape or ruler
One pair of scissors
Half a dozen pins
One sewing needle
Thread of approximately the same colour as the material in the trousers

How to Do It

1) Ideally, you will probably want your trousers to be sitting on your shoes without flopping all the way over on to the ground. Put your trousers on and stand in front of a mirror. Bend over and fold the excess on the trouser leg up inside the leg. You may have to make several adjustments to get the bottom of the trouser leg sitting just as you want it.

2) Once you are happy with the leg length (remember that some new trousers and jeans may 'ride up' a bit with wear, so you might want to leave just a little more sitting on your shoe than you might ideally like), bend down and pin the hem in place. Stick each pin through from the outside to the inside, horizontally along the hem, then force the point back out again. Repeat this half a dozen times.

3) Take your trousers off and turn them inside out. Make sure the fold is even. You can now remove the pins.

4) With your ironing board at the ready, iron the temporary hem in place.

5) Decide how deep you want the hem to be. You don't want it to be more than about two inches (5cm) or less than about one inch (2½cm). Cut away any excess to leave you a manageable hem to work with.

6) Thread your needle. You need to pull about four inches (10cm) of thread through the needle and you will have to remember to clamp this half-loop of thread in your fingers as you sew to avoid unthreading the needle.

7) Now unravel about 18 inches (45cm) of thread from the reel and cut it off. Tie a knot in the end of the thread, large enough so that, when you start sewing, the thread is not pulled out of the material.

8) Push the needle through the hem from the outside (which will be the inside once the trouser leg has been turned right-way round), near the cut-off edge, and draw the thread up to the knot. Start at one of the trouser seams, not in the middle.

9) Close to where the thread exits the hem, use the point of the needle to catch a few threads of the material of the trouser leg. Don't push the needle all the way through the material, as then the hem stitches would be visible. Draw the thread tight, and repeat the process about half an inch (just over 1cm) along the hem. Repeat until you have stitched the entire hem.

10) When you have finished, push the needle through the hem and, as you draw the thread tight, push the needle through the contracting loop to make a knot.

You have now completed one hem and can turn your trousers right way out again. Compare the first leg with the second to measure off how much you need to fold up inside the second leg to make the hem flap – most people, after all, have both legs roughly the same length.

How to Sew On a Button

An otherwise eminently smart appearance can be ruined by a missing or hanging button. Rectifying the situation is simplicity itself.

What You'll Need

One button, preferably the original or one matching it

A sewing needle
Thread
Scissors

How to Do It

1) It is worth taking the time to find a button that matches the others and a thread of a colour that blends with the fabric and the button itself.

2) Cut a length of thread just over a foot (30cm) long.

3) Thread the needle. You'll need good light and patience. Getting in a temper when the eyehole won't take the thread is a sure-fire way to prick your finger. Wet the thread with some spittle to ease the threading process.

4) With the needle securely half way along the thread, tie a knot at one end. You may need to double knot to make it really secure.

5) With the button in place where it is to be sewn, push the needle up through the material and one of the button holes. Pull it all the way through so that the thread is anchored in the fabric behind the button by the knot you tied.

6) Now push the needle through the next hole on the button and back through the fabric. Don't pull too hard as you want your button to have a bit of slack.

7) Most buttons have either two or four holes. You should aim to carry out steps 5) and 6) around three times for each hole to make sure the button is properly secured with several strands of thread.

8) End your sewing with the needle on the underside of the fabric. Secure any loose thread with a double knot.

How to Darn a Sock

A skill virtually lost to the modern world, darning can save you if you find a small 'potato' in one of your favourite pairs of socks.

What You'll Need

A hole-y sock
A darning needle
Yarn
A light bulb

How to Do It

1) Find a yarn that reasonably matches the colour of your sock and the texture of the material.

2) Thread your needle. A darning needle is considerably bigger than an ordinary one so this bit

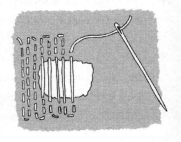

should be relatively easy. Nor need you worry about knotting either end once the yarn is threaded.

3) Insert a light bulb into the sock so that you can see its surface through the hole to be darned. This will give you some shape to work with.

4) Put a few running stitches in the sock, starting about ½ inch (1.25cm) to the side of the hole. Running stitches are small, even stitches that catch in and out of a piece of fabric. When you have finished one row, double back the yarn on itself and insert another row next to the first. Up the number of running stitches per row the closer you get to the hole.

5) Once you reach the hole, you want to 'bridge' it with the yarn. Weave in the yarn from about half an inch below the hole and continue the stitch for about half an inch above it. When you have completed the first row over the hole, double back and put in another. Don't pull the yarn too tight as this will distort the shape of the sock.

6) When the entire hole and a further half inch of material on the other side is covered with these vertical stitches, cut the end of the yarn.

7) Now start darning the yarn crossways over the hole, weaving over and under the existing threads.

8) Continue back and forth until the hole has disappeared. Trim off any excess thread.

And Finally . . .

The expression 'Experience is the best teacher' is a cliché precisely because it is true. Any adventurous-minded, self-reliant, independent sort of chap knows that competence comes from knowledge, experience, and a hefty measure of common sense. He will also know, approve of, and apply the sound old military maxim that 'Time spent in reconnaissance is seldom wasted.'

To that end, he will seek out and devour books and articles on many of the subjects covered in this book, about anything from the identification of edible plants (including fungi, a few of which are extremely poisonous) or techniques for finding fresh water, to navigation and self-defence. In many cases, he will undertake some of the professionally run courses in subjects from advanced driving to life-saving and on to first aid and essential survival skills, gaining qualifications that might one day save his, or someone else's, life. All he needs to find these are two remarkable institutions: a public library, and the Internet (the one often being available in the other).

Thus armed, he will be able to confront any unexpected situation with coolness and common sense – and on the way, will find that his own adventures have become all the more satisfying and enjoyable.